Improving Teaching and Learning *in* SCHOOLS and Colleges

George P. Waldheim, Ed.D.

Improving Teaching and Learning in the Schools and Colleges

Copyright 2016, Author: Dr. George P. Waldheim, Paradise, California. USA

ISBN: 978-0-9974310-3-2 E-book
ISBN: 978-0-9974310-4-9 Paperback
ISBN: 978-0-9974310-5-6 Hardcover

First Published in the United States in 2017, all rights reserved. No part of this publication may be reproduced distributed in any form or by any means, or stored in a data base or retrieval system, without the prior written permission of the author. E-mail: towally@comcast.net.

Book and cover design: Debbi Stocco, MyBookDesigner.com

Printed in the United States

This publication is designed to provide information for all concerned people who are committed to significantly improving teaching and learning in schools and colleges. It is published under the expressed understanding that any decisions or actions taken as a result of reading this publication must be based on your personal judgement and will be at your sole risk. The author will not be held responsible for the consequences of any actions and/or decisions taken as a result of any information given or recommendations made.

Dedication

This book is dedicated to helping those students who struggle to learn in the traditional classroom environment and to those teachers, administrators, and all concerned people who are committed to significantly improving the learning of others—thus the prescriptive work: *"Improving Teaching and Learning in Schools and Colleges."*

Table of Contents

Dedication.. iii
Acknowledgements vii
Author Biography.. ix
Preface xi
Introduction 1
Chapter 1: Current Teaching and Learning 7
    The Situation 7
    A Thought.. 15
    Improvements: Current Teaching and Learning.............. 16
Chapter 2: Teacher Responsibility and Accountability 17
    The Need 17
    Developing an Interest to Learn........................... 25
    A Thought.. 28
    Improvements: Teacher Responsibility and Accountability..... 29
Chapter 3: Teaching Methodologies 31
    Ensuring Learning 31
    A Thought.. 39
    Improvements: Ensure Learning 41
Chapter 4: Teacher Preparation 43
    The Learning Plan 43
    Topic Objectives 44
    Methods of Instruction................................... 46
    Analysis of Learning 48
    Improvement 50
    A Thought.. 52
    Improvements: Teacher Preparation....................... 53
Chapter 5: Teacher Evaluation.................................. 55
    The Process.. 55
    A Thought.. 63
    Improvements: Teacher Evaluation 65
Chapter 6: Teacher Contracts................................... 67
    Types and Content 67
    A Thought.. 76
    Improvements: Teacher Contracts 78

Chapter 7: Teacher Education 81
   Programs and Learning 81
   What Teacher Education Programs Traditionally Focus On 82
   What Teacher Education Programs Should Focus On 84
   Interpreting Student Test Results 86
   A Thought.. 89
   Improvements: Teacher Education........................ 90

Chapter 8: Eliminating Gender Bias 91
   Teaching and Gender Bias 91
   A Thought.. 97
   Improvements: Eliminate Gender Bias 98

Chapter 9: Management of Teachers 99
   The Processes... 99
   A Logical Thought 100
   Final Examinations.................................... 102
   Current Faculty Evaluation 103
   Important Concepts 106
   A Thought... 107
   Improvements: Management of Teachers 109

Chapter 10: Ethics and Teaching 111
   Responsibilities 111
   Improvements: Ethics and Teaching 113

Chapter 11: Improving Schools and Colleges 115
   Current Teaching and Learning (Chapter 1)................ 115
   Teacher Responsibility and Accountability (Chapter 2)....... 116
   Teaching Methodologies (Chapter 3).................... 117
   Teacher Preparation (Chapter 4)........................ 117
   Teacher Evaluation (Chapter 5) 118
   Teacher Contracts (Chapter 6) 118
   Teacher Education (Chapter 7)......................... 119
   Eliminating Gender Bias (Chapter 8).................... 120
   Management of Teachers (Chapter 9) 120
   Ethics and Teaching (Chapter 10) 121
   A Final Thought 121

Acknowledgements

I acknowledge that the initial motivation to write this book was generated by the experiences and suggestions relayed to me by so many current and prior students, teachers, and administrators. The commonality of both their experiences and mine, coupled with a mutual intent for significant improvement, served as incentive for this "treatise."

It is without hesitation that I acknowledge the significant support of my wife Carol, and daughters Kate & Marjorie, and their unending commitment to helping others learn.

Finally, a written response, **"Improving Teaching and Learning in Schools and Colleges,"** to all those who I have encountered who lamented the tribulations of learning and their desire for a better experience.

Thanks to all!

Author Biography

Professional Experience

The author taught and managed in various environments including the military, business and industry, teacher education, and public colleges/universities. The positions included: Sergeant-US Marine Corps Training Command, Co-owner of a Manufacturing Company in Buffalo NY, Associate Professor at the University of Nebraska-Omaha/Lincoln NE, Professor and Department Chair at California State University-Chico CA, Dean of Business and Technology at College of the Redwoods-Eureka CA, and Dean of the College of Technology at Ferris State University-Big Rapids MI.

Education

Associate Degree from Erie County Technical Institute (currently Erie Community College) Williamsville NY, Bachelor and Master of Science Degrees in Education from Buffalo State College-State University of New York (SUNY)-Buffalo NY, Doctorate in Education from the University at Buffalo (SUNY)-Buffalo NY.

Service and Awards

Rotarian-Eureka CA, President-Small Business Development Center (SBDC) Humboldt and Del Norte Counties-CA, Vice-President-CA Community Colleges Association of Occupational

Education (CCCAOE) North/Far North Region, Chair-CA North Coast Articulation Council, Accreditation Reviewer for Northwest Association of Schools and Colleges-Seattle WA.

"Award of Excellence" for outstanding achievement in education, research, and service to students—Halliburton Education Foundation, University of Nebraska. Awarded "Professor Emeritus" California State University-Chico. Prior professional memberships: Society of Manufacturing Engineers (SME), Chair-American Society for Engineering Education (ASEE) Midwest Section Engineering Technology Division, National Assoc. of Industrial Technology(NAIT).

PREFACE

To: Teachers, Students, Supervisors/Administrators, Lawmakers, and the General Public.

Why a book on "Improving Teaching and Learning in Schools and Colleges?

The international ranking of the United States (U.S.) in education is "mediocre" yet the U.S. is the world's leader in manufacturing, military, food production, space exploration, etc. The U.S. high school "dropout" rate is extremely high and reported SAT test scores (college admissions) are inexplicably low. Depending upon where the information comes from, the government or the private sector, the reported current number of high school dropouts in the U.S. is approximately 3 million plus students per year. This number, actually a slight improvement over previous years, amounts to about *8,300 students dropping out each day.* In addition there are the unreported "stay-outs;" those who have gone through the system, survived bad learning experiences, and have vowed to never return unless forced—in many cases a requirement of employment prevails. Their number is indeterminable, but they present a strong force in public discussion concerning their questionable classroom memories. Put together, dropouts and stay-outs, that's an awful lot of potential learners who have called it quits on the U.S. system of education.

There is both public and political agreement that the U.S.

system of public education has discernible problems and band-aid improvements such as new programs and more dollars are not improving student learning. Critics of education are profound in emphasizing that prior national incentive type initiatives have not significantly improved the education dilemma. Unfortunately, that perception is somewhat accurate in that the U.S. continues to maintain a mediocre international education ranking, low SAT scores, high dropout rates and an indeterminable number of dissatisfied stay-outs. Critics also point to the difference in teaching practices employed in the "world of education" courses versus the more effective practices employed in "real world" related courses. In the "world of education" the emphasis is on teaching: expecting students to learn the way the teacher teaches, emphasizing a single-mode of learning (hearing via lecture) with teacher accountability justified by a diverse spread of student grades—depicting high grade reward and low grade penalty. Whereas in the "real world" the emphasis is on learning: expecting teachers to teach the way students learn, emphasizing the multi-modes of learning (hearing, seeing, feeling) with teacher accountability justified by continuously analyzing learning for re-teaching and improvement—producing higher/less diverse grades and easier learning for all.

Therefore, to improve the level of student learning in schools and colleges and position the U.S. as a leader in world education, educators need to significantly improve the way students are taught including: teacher preparation, teaching methodologies, analysis of learning, and continuous improvement.

Purpose

The purpose of this book is to improve teaching and learning in schools and colleges in the United States. The format will be to first analyze problems that deter students from learning, in many cases regress learning, and then present "real world" proven solutions. These solutions are intended to improve teaching and learning and establish a system based on analysis of learning and continuous improvement. Therefore, in the spirit of improvement, many educationally deficient practices will be discussed in great length; not as an adversary of and/or to former colleagues who have been some of the finest and educationally committed teachers and administrators in our country. Again, this book is written in the spirit of significantly improving current educational practices, thus improving student learning in our public schools and colleges.

The final portions of this book will focus on improving supervisory and administrative responsibilities. This includes the implementation of procedures necessary to manage and maintain continuous improvement. Relative to all of this will be the application of the problem-solving concept that to change something or someone, we have to change ourselves first in order to illicit a responding change. The key is what the current education system will have to change to significantly improve student learning. **That is what this book is all about!**

Note: The improvement practices described in this text realistically will be accomplished over time, beginning in the classroom with those most importantly related to multi-learning mode teaching, analysis of learning, and continuous improvement.

Introduction

My name is Dr. George P. Waldheim. I spent the first half of my career in private business plant operations, recognizing and solving problems. The second half was in public education, watching "teaching and learning" problems develop and magnify in a system unwittingly structured to minimize improvement. Specifically, 18 years in manufacturing, both labor and management, and 22 years in education, both teaching and administration. Educationally, I have an Associate, Bachelor and Master of Science Degrees, and a Doctorate Degree in Education. Professionally, I began teaching in the Military; afterwards teaching and administering a wide variety of classes from church school to two-year College, four-year College, and then the University. Additionally, I received a Halliburton Foundation "Award of Excellence in Education" and also served as a Coordinator of College Admissions, Academic Standards, and Advisement; an Accreditation Reviewer for a

National-Regional Accreditation Commission, a Department Chair responsible for a number of faculty, a College Dean responsible for faculty and programs, and subsequently a University Dean. Personally, my wife and I have parented two children from kindergarten to college. I know what it is to be a parent concerned about the education of children.

A Real World Comparison

In the Real World: "We pay a seller for the product they sell. If their product does not work, we get it repaired/replaced, or get our money back."

In Public Education: "We pay a teacher to learn what they teach. If the learning is poor, we are penalized with a low grade and lose our money."

Analysis: "To the public this does not make sense, is illogical, and appears to unjustly justify poor learning."

Current Reality

In business, when problems occur with a product, they have to be solved. If the problems are not solved the product becomes unmarketable and the business loses money. If the business loses too much money it goes out of business, so the emphasis has to be on solving problems in order to keep the product current, marketable, and to stay in business. In education, when problems occur with the most important product, *student learning,* the current response appears to illogically blame it on the consumer, the student; they

INTRODUCTION

don't listen, they don't do the work, etc. A strong public perception is that educators do not attempt any teaching practice/process changes necessary to "fix" the learning problems by alluding to their long stated justification— "we have no control over what the student does." Again the teaching practices are repeated all over with a new class or semester. Minimal thought is given to resolving the problem of poor student learning except to issue poor grades. The reality appears to be that the public education institution does not go out of business when the product depreciates thus the problems only persist, and time evolves, and the end result is a matter of public record—student learning does not significantly improve.

Therefore, the sole purpose of this book is to examine ineffective teaching practices and recommend the changes, more so the methodology improvements, necessary to replace those ineffective practices and make the U.S. a world leader in education. To accomplish this will require implementing both the "millennium proven" practices of effective teaching" and the "real world" proven processes of analysis and continuous improvement with the goal of significantly increasing student learning and reducing the dropout rate to a lower structural level; that is students moving in and out of the system due to family/personal relocation versus the current disaster.

The difference between students dropping out of school or being a success in school is, more often than not, directly related to the teaching/learning system. Their decision, to stay or leave, is based on what they experience. Simply put, with good experiences they tend to stay, with too many bad experiences they go! Good, coupled with bad, students "learn" to tolerate current teaching and discouragement in order to graduate. Rest assured improvement in education is not a one-time solution, or specifically, more money related. It is a teaching-learning related issue and improvement will require changes in practices that are traditionally "difficult" to discuss. It will take many process changes to improve, but collectively it will redirect a system that admittedly can never be perfect, but can and will be one of the best in the world.

A THOUGHT

How did transportation go from the early bare bones cars to the luxurious models of today? How did medicine go from treating the cause to preventing the cause? How did communications go from the radio to multi-mode information technology? How did. . . . .? Answer: by analyzing what was produced and continuously improving it for ever changing needs—physical, technological, and societal!

Now, how did education go from the early 1900's teacher standing in front of a class preach-teaching—to today's teacher standing in front of a class preach-teaching? This was accomplished because in the public teaching system there is not a common and/or effective process that documents the classroom product produced (level of student learning) specifically for analysis and continuous improvement. This situation, *over time,* not only facilitates but perpetuates poor learning.

Individuals in the teaching profession are becoming increasingly aware that students and the general public are considering themselves to be front line consumers and thus perceive they

Introduction

have a purchaser's right of inquiry and logical obligation to hold their school board, administrators, and faculty accountable for the productivity of their product—"student learning." An example: When the public purchases food *all* the product ingredients (nutrition facts) and performance level of the product (calories) are lawfully revealed for their decision making. When the public purchases education the specific course ingredients (information expectations) and performance level (instructional effectiveness) are generally unavailable.

It is becoming an ever-increasing reality that the funding parties (both government and public) expect the course ingredients and the performance level of instruction for effective planning and decision-making. *Therefore, to be sure the public and the U.S. system of education have the most effective course ingredients and performance levels will require implementing both the "millennium proven" practices of effective teaching and the "real world" proven processes of analysis and continuous improvement—well described in this book.*

The questions most persistently asked about improving education are: **What do we need? Why don't we have it? How can we get it? Read On!**

Chapter 1: Current Teaching and Learning

The Situation

To improve teaching and learning it is important to first examine current teaching practices and the effects they have on student learning.

Therefore, If the student doesn't learn, let's not be so quick to blame the student! Most students who initially enter a class have the mental disposition to want to complete and/or do well in the class. Those who enter a class with a preconceived notion of difficulty or failure have already contracted that notion from previous bad learning experiences. Thus it appears it would be the education system's responsibility to "repair," however instead of repairing and restoring those relationships the traditional practice appears to justify the student's future difficulty or failure by relating to their past performance. Therefore, "It is not our fault" so students are advised to go somewhere else or given their well-deserved "F."

This "kick the can down the road" solution to the problem tends to get worse and results in greater student alienation of the system; more dropouts and more stay-outs!

An overwhelming number of community college students, when interviewed, expressed similar experiences. First, they did poorly in high school because it was just not interesting, didn't make sense, and "they did not learn well." Additionally, they felt the teacher ignored them and gave the attention to the better learners. Thus, they developed a poor perception of themselves; some to the point they remembered being told, "It's too bad you can't learn." Now, later in life, they realize, mostly because of success in their job, they can learn and they come back to school in spite of the prior damage inflicted. Unfortunately, recognizable damage is done in the educational system and this is the direct result of poor teaching practices. Had the teacher been directly responsible for analyzing what the students should have learned, the problem being exposed by low test scores (measured course objectives), and given other necessary improvements in the system that will be discussed later, those problems would have been prevented from repeating themselves. However, situations like this persist, magnify, and tend to go on year after year. When returning students are interviewed, the same names of the teachers inflicting the damage re-occur.

Many older adults still have nightmares about a class, or classes, they took 20, 30, to even 40 or 50 years ago. When asked, "Was it interesting, make sense, give you the feeling of accomplishing learning that will help you?" They laughed and said, "Just the opposite!" For too many students the educational system did more "perception" damage than good. The community college enrollments are filled with students whose prior education experience (elementary and high school) was much less than satisfactory.

It is necessary to change the current teaching practices if we want to become a world leader in education. Specifically, to change and improve the level of student learning means improving the way students are taught! Note: In the classroom there is only a teacher and the students. Theoretically, if we take away the teacher then no learning occurs. Therefore, the teacher, when teaching, causes learning to take place. **The level of this learning can and should be documented; it is the baseline for instructional improvement.** Learning happens in an environment of varying applications of student abilities, interests, dispositions, feelings, etc., much of which is in reaction to the teaching. If teaching is *improved* then student learning is improved, as well as the student perception and value of learning. Only then will the U.S. be able to reduce the dropout and stay-out rates, and be able to change an educational system currently focused on other priorities in lieu of student learning.

Be aware: Today's teaching is *too significantly* based on what can be characterized as "verbal lecture" (expounding, urging, telling). To the counter-argument "not necessarily so because we use computers," the reply is No! Computers, currently and for the most part, have not changed the lecture methodology. Students *read* the computer screen, on which they are seeing words/numbers etc., and then go about repeating it to themselves as if they heard it from the lecturer's mouth; thus the students are lecturing to themselves.

Now, how effective is the "lecture" method? Look at your life situations. As a parent I told them not to do it but they just won't listen. As a friend I warned them but they just didn't listen. As a whatever, you get the point! Isn't the way information is sent, received, and **learned** dramatically different today than it was verbally 30, 20, or even a few years ago? If so, why haven't we dramatically changed the way we teach? *In the spirit of answering this question it is necessary to first ask ourselves: How do I* **remember** *things best? By Hearing it? Seeing it? or Doing it? The answer exposes the dilemma: U.S. schools and colleges are not teaching to the way students learn (remember things best). This is the very nature of our student learning problem.*

Teaching, *mostly* by verbal lecturing, is deficient (lacking the additional modes of learning) and persists in schools and colleges. This occurs due to the educational system's traditional evaluation practices and thus unwittingly protects this deficient teaching methodology. Additionally there is a system wide lack of requiring analysis of learning for planning continuous improvement—even when justified by obvious and documented "poor student learning."

Do you want to know who the better, *not necessarily the most effective*, teachers are? Just ask the students! They know because they are the products being produced. They have the real experience of what is being learned and at what level. Others, for the most part, do not! As an example: One institution's school bookstore had its glass windows completely covered with each faculty member's previous class student evaluation summary page. The students would read the scores and make decisions on what classes to take, based on the scores. The next semester all evaluation summaries were removed and thus the problems hidden. In reality, it is a fact that **the public is paying for learning** and logically has an invested right to see what they get for their money. In reality, the current teaching accountability *practice* appears to be quite dissimilar to the way it was hundreds of years ago because then the teachers/lecturers would walk down an aisle and the students would put teaching payment money in the frock-tail rear pouch of their lecture robe. The teacher/lecturer would be paid according to their student's perception of their performance. Next time you go to a graduation ceremony look closely at the frock-tail of the faculty robes that are suspended from the around their necks. You will see the characteristic rear pouch, most likely now a ceremonial dress tradition. Makes one well aware that years ago teachers were more accountable for student learning because payment was directly related to their performance; that is, how the students perceived their *learning*—was it worth it or not? Today, in reverse, *student learning is held accountable* by critical ranges of grades given by the teacher. *In effect this has not promoted teaching motivation.* It appears this whole reversal in roles occurred because teachers are employed by bureaucratic entities such as a town, city, state, etc. rather than directly by the students. Therefore, accountability for student learning was shifted to the students and evolved away from the teacher. This reversal in accountability, now a tradition, has resultant effects on student learning!

So for now, the current teaching and learning system is not able to respond with continuous instructional improvement to measured student learning. In fact, as outlined in the following chapters, the system hides the problems and even promotes the extension of them. Teachers will have to improve the system to first evaluate at what level the students have learned the class material, and second, if the learning is low or unacceptable, make immediate changes to the methods of instruction in order to improve learning. The important point will be the level of student learning considered acceptable; not grades on any curve, but a straightforward score and documentation of what the student has learned in the class versus what the student was supposed to have learned in that class. *All subjects included!* Actually, many "real world" related educators have been doing that for years. Their programs have measurable objectives and standards that must be demonstrated by testing in order for the student to continue in the program. Unfortunately, accountability for what *all* the students should have learned is not part of the current teaching employment system. Take note that the current system, because of verbal lecture (expounding, urging, telling), caters to only those learners *who more naturally* absorb enough information *heard* from the lecturer to pass informational tests on the lecture and move on in the system. This selective teaching practice (verbal lecture) is deceptively justified by the use of statistical sampling whereby the student's grades are analyzed on a graphically shaped curve (example: graphically plotting test letter grades versus number of students attaining those grades). The deception is the inference drawn from the grades: the high grades are inferred to represent high student effort/learning and the low grades, unjustifiably and unfortunately, just the opposite. **In reality, the grades more logically represent the varying strengths of individual students'**

modes of learning—Hearing, Seeing, and Feeling. Those few whose natural receptive learning mode for lecture (Hearing) is very strong will tend to be at the positive tail of the curve (high grades) whereas those few with very poor receptivity to lecture, more naturally receptive to the other modes, will tend to be at the negative tail of the curve (low grades). The larger remaining group (varying and less biased modes of learning) appear in the center top and both descending sides of a resultant bell shaped curve. In reality, this deceptive process of grade interpretation appears to justify low grades by relating them to low effort/learning; thus the failure of those who do not naturally learn well from "lecturing!" Which, as described before, is an awful lot of people!

Important: When a teacher plans and teaches using all the learning receptivity modes: Hearing (verbal), Seeing (visual), and Feeling (application), of their students, with the intent that they all must learn; the results destroy the aforementioned curve, the grading inferences, and the justification for selective teaching by verbal lecture. It is teaching directed to all students, by utilizing all the learning receptivity modes to acquire knowledge. The only variables remaining are the differences in the individual levels of information retention; *they all were able to receive and process the information*, but retained it at different levels. Logically the graded scores would be higher because more students receive/process the information; thus—**more learn easier!**

Case in point: An administrator reviews a class grade sheet at the end of the semester and asked why the teacher had no failures, with the expectation that there should have been some. The teacher told him/her the way he/she taught was to ensure all students learned the information at an acceptable level, as documented by measured course objectives, and thus no failures! The teacher destroyed the curve by teaching to each student's mode of learning, ensuring their receptivity of the required subject matter and that was reflected in the testing results and subsequent grades. The administrator did not question the answer but the teacher could tell that the administrator was disturbed by it and that only reinforces the argument as to the accepted regimentation of a system that is ill equipped to accept the notion that the only failure in the classroom is the teacher. Remember, curve reported learning all goes back to the current teaching method which is most generally "verbal lecture." In actuality, the students are being graded on only how well they adapted to the verbal lecturing and those that do not are eliminated from the system by low grades, dropping out, or staying out! If the whole notion of verbal teaching today is questionable, remember "I told him/her not to do it but they just didn't listen," then what about the evaluation stemming from that, and the advisement, and so on?

Years later those eliminated from the system tend to come back and do very well, many in similar classrooms, and the rhetoric/justification is they are more "mature now." More accurately they were disinterested because of deficient teaching (not on their wavelength); resultantly the topics did not make sense, they didn't understand/retain it, and because of all that they were perceived as poor students. So, the following chapters will examine the changes needed to improve the system and make the U.S. a world leader in education. These changes will no doubt be seen as contrary to the current status quo and be a challenge to those resistant to improving traditional teaching methods. When a student leaves school, they find out real quick that for most employment in our society they are held accountable for their performance. Teaching resulting in poor student learning cannot be acceptable in an educational system accountable to the public. It is time to start making the instructional changes to base a system on continuously improving student learning as the main objective. **How? Read on!**

A THOUGHT

To teach to all students, utilizing all three modes of learning receptivity, requires necessary and comprehensive pre-preparation by the teacher. Because of a lack of pre-preparation this methodology *rarely occurs* and the traditional practice is to assign student homework—*conceptually in error!* In reality, the homework is nothing more than the same "verbal-learning" mode of teaching (students *hearing* themselves read) emphasizing the deceptive practice that more verbal learning is better **for all.** This practice is only positive reinforcement to those biased towards the Hearing mode of learning receptivity but *conceptually in error* by actually promoting negative learning reinforcement to those more receptive to the Seeing and Feeling modes. Because the homework is not on their "wavelength" (even more difficult to learn at home than in class) those not as receptive to the Hearing mode struggle and become *much more perceptively discouraged and disinterested*, thus they dropout or survive with low grades and become a stay-out. This is where the teacher "fails" the student. I do not mean by giving them an "F," although that may be a consequence of such deceptive and deficient teaching. **Teaching incorporating all three modes of learning for all course objectives must be a religious part of classroom instruction and is the teacher's "homework" responsibility.**

Think about this: An obvious fact is those stay-outs who learned to survive in the current system, in spite of the aforementioned deficient teaching, have displayed and proven an exceptionally strong commitment to "want to learn." Who is the real failure in their classroom?

IMPROVEMENTS: CURRENT TEACHING AND LEARNING

- ▶ Teachers and administrators accept responsibility and accountability for analyzing student learning for improvement of instruction.
- ▶ Limit selective teaching by "verbal lecture" (expounding, urging, telling).
- ▶ Teach by ethically utilizing all three modes of learning receptivity for all course objectives.
- ▶ Develop student interest in all the subjects taught in the classroom.
- ▶ Promote student accomplishment for all students in the classroom.
- ▶ Measure, grade, and analyze student learning thus documenting teaching effectiveness.

Chapter 2: Teacher Responsibility and Accountability

The Need

In order to improve teaching and learning it is necessary for teachers to understand and be accountable for their foremost job responsibility—student learning!

It is a misleading statement to say the foremost responsibility of a teacher is to teach. Unfortunately, in daily usage, the verb "teach" has become more a figure of speech used to represent too many differing perceptions, camouflaging the teaching profession from its foremost responsibility. Theoretically, one can teach and give instruction but that in no way ensures learning; this is the nature of the problem in our educational system. So, how is the verb "teach" defined? Dictionary examples include "to impart knowledge," "to bestow," "to give instruction," or more specifically, "to cause to learn." The real message, in the definition of the verb "teach," is that something happens because of it! Teachers are imparting, bestowing, giving, etc. *So, how well are teachers imparting, bestowing, giving, etc., or how well are students learning?* What is the ultimate logical outcome of the process of teaching? It must be "student learning!" That is the very reason teachers are teaching; so students learn. Now, one can teach until the equator freezes but if the students do not learn the teaching effort is in vain. To be clearer: *The teacher's foremost responsibility is, and has to be, student learning!*

Now, what does the teacher have to do to promote and ensure "student learning?" To start, the teacher has to ask and answer the question: Student learning of what? A necessary part of ensuring learning is that all major topics of instruction, therein to be learned, should be documented by learning objectives and a corresponding method of measuring student accomplishment of those objectives. Note: For the purpose of this discussion, the word "objective" is a noun and refers to that which is created by the teacher, and then is worked for to achieve. The definition of the word "goal" is for defining the overall purpose of a course of instruction. In essence, the overall course will have a goal, and subsequent to that, the informational topics necessary to reach that goal will be made up of cumulative measurable objectives.

Measurable Objectives: How can teachers tell if the learners have met the topic objectives if they cannot be measured or if the objectives just plain do not exist? If learner accomplishment of individual topic objectives cannot be measured, then teachers cannot document if learning of those objectives actually took place, at what level, and the effectiveness of the teaching. *Whatever material is being taught, it should be derived, planned, and implemented with measurable objectives and the evaluation results analyzed to document the effectiveness of the teaching—as well as being used as the basis for subsequent improvements.* Yes, some courses and/or subjects currently have measurable objectives in place, but unfortunately too many do not!

To those critics who say "Where have you been?" The response is:

Let's see the levels of effectiveness of teaching at your institution documented by class grade averages based on comprehensive final examinations or cumulative tests, grading all course objectives; all students—no exemptions.

Let's see a comparison of the teaching at your institution, relative to teacher effectiveness, as documented by class grade averages based on...

Let's see your institution's minimum acceptable level of teaching effectiveness, relative to student learning, as documented by class grade averages based on...

Typical responses are: "Yes, the public is paying to learn but performance levels are confidential!" Yet in the real world we can easily find graded performance levels of most products/services on the Internet—*before* purchasing them. In public education, after the class is paid for and over, it is hidden. *This makes the public wonder why—and thus suspicious!*

Now, think of this: If the class comprehensive final examination grades, for all the students in the class, show half of the class received grades of C and above, and the other half received grades of C and below, that would indicate a lower level of student learning versus a similar class showing all C's and above. This process would reveal the level of learning that took place, relative to the course objectives, and thus the effectiveness of the teaching and necessity for improvement.

Concerned critics ask: What is the minimum acceptable level of teacher effectiveness for a class, relative to documented student learning, at your school/institution? Not sure? Educational institutions are always concerned about student learning but when it is tied to teacher effectiveness they tend to respond unknowing! Without documenting the effectiveness of teaching, there can be little accountability to the job responsibility of "student learning." Little accountability reflects little improvement and/or complacency; this is the current situation.

If teachers want to improve education, it is necessary to document how effective their teaching currently is, based on documented student learning, and then analyze the learning and implement a continuous process of instructional improvement. Teachers must be able to show where they currently are, and then, where they are going. Doing this learning improves! Not doing this learning regresses!

Getting back to course objectives: For the most part math, science, and other "real world" related courses appear to be somewhat compliant; most often due to certification, registration, or other institutional, commercial, or standardized testing requirements. These entities, for the most part, require documentation of a student's performance. Generally, during institutional accreditation review, courses and related instructional material do identify a course goal and then define *minimal* general objectives to meet that goal. Examples of student performance (generalized testing) are usually provided to the reviewer with other course related materials, many times voluminous. *Please note:* **In too many cases, cumulative topical measurable objectives for entire courses and corresponding methods of documenting student performance of those objectives does not exist.** Usually, just a couple of course cover sheets indicating the goal of the course and a few stated objectives relative to that goal, including a grading system for the course and other class information relating to attendance, assignments, etc. In the minimal of cases where strong documentation exists, verifying topic objectives and performance assessment of those objectives, they are mostly presented by teachers who had significant experience in business, science, health, technology, engineering or other "real world" occupations before teaching.

The problem in education is that there is not an accountable method to promote this "assurance of performance," for *both* teacher and student, other than a final course grade which in too many instances is derived from data far removed from actual measurable performance of course objectives. Think about it, if a teacher presents a topic and then assesses the learning of that topic, the outcome of the assessment not only documents student learning, but also and more importantly, the effectiveness of the teaching. At that point, the teacher should determine what changes have to be made to increase student learning for that topic objective. The changes include re-teaching the topic after improving the instructional methodology, etc. The important point being the teacher now knows how effective their teaching was and now has the improvement opportunity to determine what changes they have to make to assure an acceptable or increased level of student learning. Unfortunately testing is viewed as a threat by students and is generally ignored by teachers as an assessment of a teacher's effectiveness. The very nature and culture of this philosophy has to be changed in order to increase and assure student learning.

It is a teacher's responsibility to clearly design, draft, and document all course major topics with written measurable objectives. Complimentary, the teacher must develop and document objective ways to measure the student performance of those topic objectives. This is a comprehensive task and generally avoided because of the work involved. Unfortunately, too many teachers take the easy way out, and leave this task to the writers of related course texts and test questions at the end of the textbook chapters. This is a good example of what not to do! Textbooks are written in specific readable format and are a good tool to accompany a teacher's informational format but are not, and should not, be the course inclusive. To do this is to lose the advantage of individualized instruction; related material developed and presented in a multi-mode format by a teacher who is familiar with the varying learning characteristics of the students in the class. The course topic objectives and the methods to teach and measure the accomplishment of those objectives should relate to the specific student group, in a person-to-person class setting.

Note that some state and national "standardized testing" requirements may persuade teachers to identify measureable objectives for all the major topics being taught in their course. This probably would occur out of a teacher's necessity to respond to whatever results are identified by standardized testing. If standardized test scores are low, the institution response may be "poor student performance" whereas the student/parent response may be "poor teaching." *In either case, the learning level of the students and the effectiveness of the teaching can and should be revealed by evaluating individual course objectives versus their corresponding class examination grades.* This review would identify what and where the learning problems exist and serve to justify planned improvement. If this documentation does not exist then the "disease cannot be identified and/or treated" and the patient (the student) permanently suffers (grades on transcripts do not disappear), and the problem only tends to repeat itself with a new group of students. On the other hand, high standardized test scores can be reviewed back to identify student and teacher performance, and the results used to promote even better teaching.

Critics of standardized testing strongly comment that high standardized test scores relate to the teacher teaching the test. However, it is logically accepted that standardized tests are derived from numerous individual topic objectives for the given course as identified by some outside agency: federal, state, county, etc. Actually, when you think about it, the people designing the standardized tests are identifying individual course objectives from which to formulate the standardized test. They, in fact, are doing the job the teacher should be, or should have done prior to the course being taught. Then, they are assessing student performance of those objectives just as the teacher would, or should, be doing. Had this process occurred in individual classes or courses then there would not be such a strong need for standardized testing except for academic comparisons on larger scales. Additionally, the importance of standardized testing serves to not only identify student achievement, but also document teacher effectiveness. Unfortunately, as outlined in other chapters of this text, the resolution of deficient teaching under the current operational and supervisory systems needs to be improved because it lacks an accountability process for analysis and continuous improvement. Without improvement the problems procrastinate and infect a completely new class by repeating themselves; and on and on...

If we, as a nation, want to be a leader in world education then we have to promote excellent teaching and improve ineffective teaching—all through a process of analysis of learning and continuous improvement. Standardized testing is a natural threat to those who are ineffective teachers. Remember, the only failure in the "real world" classroom is the teacher! If learning does not take place, then the "cause to learn" has been ineffective and that is one of the primary job responsibilities of the teacher. This can only be resolved through documentation and resultant change.

On the issue of standardized testing: It is apparent that there are certain subjects/courses that relate to most curriculums of study and are natural candidates for comparative type testing. Therefore it seems reasonable for educational systems to maintain similar course content in math, science, language, etc. Even the Greeks agreed on their "trivium" of lower division subjects (grammar, rhetoric, logic) thus demonstrating their educational common agreement. *It cannot be ignored that as geographically widespread the U.S. educational system is, and as competitive as the individual systems have become, there should be some commonality in courses; thus the outcomes of those common courses would necessitate documented accountability.*

Developing an Interest to Learn

What does the teacher have to do to promote student learning? In addition to documenting the learning objectives for individual courses, and the methods of measurement for documenting and analyzing the student learning of those objectives, it is a fundamental responsibility of the teacher to generate the "cause to learn." Necessity is the mother of invention; without establishing and convincing students of the necessity of learning the individual objectives it will be that much more difficult for learning to take place. People do what they tend to be interested in; if the teacher does not or cannot develop student interest in the subject matter of the topic objectives, one cannot expect students to learn just because they are told about it, or told to do it. This is one of the greatest challenges the teacher faces: determining how the individual course topic objectives meaningfully relate to the students. If a student is convinced the information presented is needed, then real learning tends to take place. If the student cannot see the need or necessity in the information, they either memorize it or just plain let it go out of the memory window. Overall, it has long been accepted there is a strong correlation between interest and learning. The teacher must develop "necessity interest" in the student if formidable learning is to take place.

How many readers of this text have sat in classes at either the elementary, secondary (high school), or college level and wondered why they were even there. Unfortunately, some whole courses are this way and they persist semester after semester. Years later, generally in the world of work, some significant happening will trigger the memory flash of that boring teacher and class with the wonderment of why the teacher did not use what just happened as an example to generate interest. Too little class preparation, too late, too little experience, or possibly the teacher just lectured and was not really interested in comprehensive "student learning." This type of teaching is what educators have to prevent in order to be the world's leader in education. In practice new teachers, those just entering the profession, tend to take more time to investigate interests and motivate their students even though they may not have significant experience in the course material. They are extremely interested in what they are doing and the impact they will make. Additionally, those new teachers, who have spent a number of years in the world of work before beginning the profession of teaching, have the advantage of experiencing real life applications of the course material and find it easier to promote student interest; convincing others of why it is important! Those professional teachers in the middle group seem to be split into two groups. Those that can create such student interest you can hear a pin drop in their class. There are "general education" teachers like this who, on occasion, have extra UN-enrolled students sitting in the aisle space of their classroom just to see, feel, and hear the topical information with their class enrolled friends because it was presented multi-mode, and thus so interesting. Then, the other type of teacher, who was just doing enough of their job to escape the wrath of a litany of complaints. All of the above situations would be clearly exposed, good or bad, by measuring student performance of individual course topic objectives to determine the level of student learning and thus the effectiveness of the teaching.

This could then be continuously analyzed by the faculty member and changes made in the methods of instruction to improve the levels of "student learning."

A final note about utilizing educational textbooks: They are an excellent source of "how to." For the most part, the authors have extensive knowledge of the material they are presenting in the text, but many times that can be a detriment instead of a help. For instance, an author who too briefly emphasizes the importance or application and spends the majority of the written material on the concept itself. This is not necessarily bad however many times it is minimally useful in the "interest promotion" process. The problem too often is that experts in their field write the texts used in courses and spend most of the text on the mechanics of whatever they are presenting. Introductory paragraphs or explanations rarely explain sufficiently and *convincingly* why and how this affects the reader and therefore does not do much to generate reader interest. The experts are so focused on the mechanics of the presentation, which rightfully is of great interest to them, the basic motivation is generally thought to be expected rather than needed to be generated. This is where the teacher must compliment the text and not ignore what seems academic to them. The writers of course texts have an extreme interest in the subject because it interests them. Such may not be the case for new learners/readers and must be significantly reinforced by the teacher. This, again, is part of course planning and takes time to develop, which is probably why it is not as common a practice as it should be. Generating student interest is the foremost promotion of learning that a teacher can make. Too many times instructional supervisors witness the converse and because of operational roadblocks built into the system (lack of necessary analysis of learning, and continuous improvement) the converse persists. There are few things more important in the responsibilities of the teacher than instilling a believable need to learn.

A THOUGHT

If the responsibility and accountability for student learning is dependent on teaching then schools and colleges can logically expect to get a greater overall teacher commitment to classroom learning. The converse is also true and is a major part of the problem preventing the U.S. from becoming the foremost leader in education in the world. Clear thinking indicates that people cannot solve problems if they don't know what they are—a perceived necessity for any improvement is truly the mother of invention; in government, business, or an educational classroom. If people have to, they will find a way to improve. If they do not have to, especially when due to a lack of accountability and continuous improvement, then complacency breeds. The unfortunate part is the student ultimately carries the consequence of complacency—poor learning. Education teachers, leaders, etc., must be responsible and accountable for what they produce!

Improvements: Teacher Responsibility and Accountability

- Accept personal and professional responsibility for student learning.
- Inspire student motivation and generate a cause to learn for all course topics.
- Create measureable objectives for all major course topics.
- Teach by ethically utilizing all three modes of learning receptivity for all course objectives.
- Document a "class grade average," grading the level of learning of all course measureable objectives and resultant teaching effectiveness, for each assigned course.
- Compute the "class grade average," using comprehensive final examination grades or cumulative test grades; all enrolled students—no exemptions.
- Prepare a continuous teaching improvement plan by analyzing the range and dispersion of test grades for individual topic objectives—versus the methods of instruction.

Chapter 3: Teaching Methodologies

Ensuring Learning

To ensure learning teachers have to begin by asking and answering the age-old questions: How do we learn? How do we know something? How do we know we know something?

What process does a learner go through to put something into their mind, then recall it from their mind, and then apply what is recalled? It would appear the whole notion of "learning" would have to include the aforementioned; putting something into one's mind, recalling it, and then applying it. One's varying ability to do that would then reflect a level of learning. Now, what is the process a learner goes through? The most accepted research on learning says people put information into their minds by various combinations of Hearing, Seeing, and/or Feeling it. Please note: just hearing, seeing, and feeling information does not in itself totally constitute learning. These are only the "modes" people use to communicate information into their, and/or others, minds. It is also accepted in teaching practice that if learners actually apply the information they heard, saw, and/or felt, they would tend to remember it better; meaning they could recall and apply it when needed—thus learned it. It would be reasonable to deduce the more times learners applied the same information they heard, saw, and/or felt, they would have "learned it" to a greater level.

The first important point in observing teaching is to examine how teachers generally go about communicating information to the student. The norm seems to be to tell it by verbal instruction (expounding, urging, telling); identified in this text as "lecture." This appears to only justify one mode of learning, *Hearing*. The *Seeing* mode is intended to be justified by visually demonstrating something related to the topic. In education, this is usually implemented by using different media mechanisms such as a white board, computer screen, etc. *Unfortunately, these mechanisms really represent the Hearing mode*—the student is repeating it to themselves, what they are reading from the board or computer, and thus hear himself or herself. The *Feeling* mode, again unfortunately and deficiently, is more often than not left out of most general education teaching—the excuse being "it does not relate well" to general education subjects except for writing as a physical application, and that is really stretching the imagination for receiving information through feeling. That is about as ineffective a representation as the whiteboard is to meeting the information receptive mode of seeing. Now, this is getting to the nature of the teaching/learning problem in our culture. Remember that *Hearing, Seeing, and Feeling* are the most accepted modes used to enter information into our minds; however, that alone does not constitute learning! We also know people naturally receive and process information at different levels of reception via the three modes. Some do well with Hearing, versus others who do better with Seeing, versus others with Feeling, even though individuals tend to use one to all three abilities combined. However, these receptive modes appear to change in priority given the situation. People tend to receive information in reaction to the way it was sent. **As an example only**: A person burning their hand on a stove will receive the burn information immediately through the feeling mode even though they may be hearing mode biased. In addition, a person's frantic motions received through the seeing mode may take precedence over a feeling bias. Overall, people tend to use the three modes to receive and process information although individually have differing, and in some cases significant personal biases, utilizing those modes. **It only makes sense individuals would receive and retain information more effectively if all three modes were used to send it. That is an important basis for effective instruction. In other words, teachers can reach more students utilizing all three receptive modes.**

In contrast, the current educational dilemma is exacerbated by the deceptive notion of success using the verbal teaching method alone (lecture-hearing). This is justified by the interpretation of test grades that plot a "bell shaped curve" thereby documenting the *"traditionally accepted learning variance"* within the class. Contrary to this notion is that those students with the stronger receptive modes of Seeing and Feeling are in trouble right from the start. This major problem has initiated many other problems in our educational system, hence those students biased in the other modes of information reception logically tend to receive lower grades, or become the students perceived as those who "just can't learn." The "just can't learn" students are usually the students who return to school after being in the world of work, finding they can learn by using the other modes of Seeing and/or Feeling; and because they were successful, why can't they go back to school and do well—in spite of the teachers. Many do, and tend to do it very well. It is apparent that the Seeing and/or Feeling biased learners have significantly experienced converting on-the-job hearing information into Seeing and/or Feeling applications at work and thus are/were more successful learning (putting information into their mind, recalling, and applying it) than they ever were at school. *They actually wound up doing the job the formal teacher should have done.* Do you see where this is heading?

Example: A new math teacher said his goal in teaching math was to take the class to the school laboratories and teach students math by showing how it is really derived and applied in real life. He said math fundamentals can and should be taught in the laboratories (applying all three receptive modes) where it is used. Incidentally, he meant real-life practical applications laboratories which his school had, not the traditional math lab with only computers programmed to reinforce the preaching methodology. This person's intent coincided with the accepted educational theory that students "can" receive information more effectively utilizing the three modes; multivariate. Also remember, "can" receive information, not saying they would receive it. What is meant by that?

Today's students appear to respond significantly different

from yesterday's students! The technology ease of making available large amounts of information has drastically changed the attention span of most people. If it interests them, they continue to read and or see on. If not, they hit "mental delete" and move on to the next item of initial interest. This conditioning directly relates to the learning behavior of the student in the classroom. If they are interested in the topic presented, and they are biased in the mode of presentation, they will probably do better than those disinterested will and/or biased otherwise. The real key here is "if they are interested." If not interested, regardless of their learning mode bias, they will probably tend to tune out the presentation and focus some of their thoughts elsewhere, not able to receive and retain enough information to start the recall and application process—learning. Since the attention span of the student today is so much shorter than that of yesteryear, it is necessary for the successful teacher to develop interest in the topic right from the start—of any concepts and/or topics they are presenting.

Teaching, according to various dictionary definitions, is "to impart knowledge" and/or "to cause to learn." Unfortunately, that is how too many teachers aggravated our learning problems: by only "imparting knowledge" through verbal lecture-hearing, all interest aside, and if students remember it okay and if not tough! Too many teachers feel their job responsibility is only to present the information and the rest is up to the individual student. If they recall it for the tests, then teachers assume they have learned it. Typical advice (unfortunate for those who are biased other than hearing) is to read it, study it, go over it many times in your mind so you remember it for the test. In today's "real world" that does not appear to work well. Attitude, time available, family structure, interest, environment, etc. are all affecting factors. To be an effective teacher one has the responsibility to impart knowledge in the most effective way, ultimately resulting in learning by the student. *Good teaching has to ensure learning.* If teachers focus on ensuring learning they can resolve the problems currently plaguing us. So, what do teachers have to do to ensure student learning?

First: Develop an interest in the required topic. Find a way to show the learner how it will affect them in an important way. One sentence as to the relevance of the topic "doesn't work!" Most people's attention is gained when the nature of the topic affects something important to them. Incidentally, threatening to give students an "F" grade does not promote interest and may actually promote the reverse. Topics necessary to be presented in classrooms or elsewhere generally have a beginning point. Someone discovered that knowledge somewhere and for some purpose of interest. Example: Where and/or **why** did the subject of Algebra develop? Where and/or **why** the Pythagorean Theorem? Where and/or **why** does a minus times a minus equal a plus, etc.? These beginning points, "where and/or **why**," are usually of interest to learners, **especially when related to "how" they seriously affect those learners today.** Another problem is that many teachers don't even know where/why/how those things were invented or developed. *It behooves the teacher to know and present real interest in the topic in order to develop a reasoning to learn.* People, even students, have to have a reason to want to do something. Learning something one sees no purpose in is a lost endeavor, defeated before starting, and much of today's verbal lecture without convincing purpose, is very successful at that!

Second: Teach all topics utilizing all three receptive modes: Hearing, Seeing, and Feeling. A lot of forethought, known as "teacher pre-preparation," will have to go into the design and implementation of this. The importance of this rule cannot be over stressed. Even if interested, if students do not receive information on their "wavelength" many will be lost and/or experience greater difficultly in learning. The person who said their elementary grade teacher was having trouble with the students understanding the process of averaging numbers gave an example of the power of all three modes. In desperation, the teacher marched the whole class to the school gym where they had the final scores of all their school's basketball games posted on the wall. The subsequent teaching and learning is obvious but the important point here was twofold. The teacher engaged the students in all three modes of learning and the result was an adult who never forgot the experience, and/or the learning that took place because of it. Another glaring example was a freshman college class in Educational Psychology 101 where the teacher gave each student the option of attending the lecture class twice a week, or going to the local halfway house for four hours per week and report writing per course instructions. Who do you think learned more about educational psychology in that class? The students at the halfway house who certainly were exposed to all three modes of learning, or those listening to the preached-hearing mode only? See the value of the three modes of perception? *Not presenting information utilizing those modes is almost derelict to the profession of teaching and certainly detrimental to the learning of the student.*

Third: Test for recall and application of each measurable objective then analyze and improve the instructional methodology, and re-teach where necessary—utilizing all three improved modes again. The given test after the teaching process is completed is not to grade the student, but to show the teacher what deficiencies exist in the methods of instruction. This gives the teacher the necessary opportunity to improve by analyzing and improving the re-teaching of those items for better student learning. It serves as a teacher self-check and is necessary for the teacher's continuous instructional improvement.

Fourth: Retest again for grading. The overall class results of the grading, personal name identification withheld, should be readily available information. It is important for a teacher to develop the mental philosophy that the only failure in the classroom will be the teacher! *It is the teacher's job to ensure learning of the students.* Effective teachers do take their responsibility personally. If students are failing in the class, then the teacher is failing. Look at all the great teachers in history. They all seem to follow the pattern of effective teaching previously outlined. They always developed interest in their various teachings which set the stage for learning. Their teachings were filled with seeing and feeling experiences, so much so that books thousands of years later still describe them. They even tested the applications of their student's learning in numerous ways.

In Schools and Colleges almost all *extremely effective* teachers have similar things in common. Their first concern is always student learning. Even the students know it—they feel it! They are hands-on, they most often develop instruction using the three modes, and their test results reflect their efforts. Few failures, if any, and always the highest perceived student evaluations. Their subjects include Math and Chemistry, traditionally known for high levels of difficulty. An example of one teacher's commitment to ensure learning was a high school chemistry classroom with the ceiling totally covered with chemical nomenclature-lattice diagrams. When asked what the ceiling diagrams were for the teacher said he told all the students if they ever fell asleep in his class the chemical designations would be the first thing they would see when their heads went upright and their eyes opened; a must in their learning! From that, those students felt and knew the teacher's commitment to their learning and developed a greater interest in the teacher and the subject. Incidentally, students know who the good teachers are, and do we really have to ask ourselves why that is?

In conclusion: In order to improve teaching and learning in America teachers must teach to ensure learning and document it! Anything less is weakening the students' opportunity to learn. *"The only failure in the classroom is the teacher."*

A THOUGHT

"How to get students to learn?" The applied psychology read, heard, seen, and actually experienced indicates that the practical answer to that question is to *change ourselves*. The reaction to *our change* tends to elicit a change in others. What is done, and how it is done motivates others—for the good or for the bad! There does not appear to be a status quo in this—things are either going positive or negative all the time. People change to elicit a corresponding change in others and when that change disappears, they are back to the original situation.

Students are much more, or significantly more, perceptive than most teachers ever give them credit for. They know and respond to the attitude, personality, and persona the teacher displays, *consciously and/or unconsciously*. Why is it that a seemingly small frail elderly teacher can hold a class of 35 plus energetic high school combined gender students spellbound and attentive versus the opposite person's physical stature, with opposite subsequent results? The students' perception of the teacher and their resultant behavior must be in reaction to whatever the teacher displays, does, or has done. A students' perception of non-verbal teacher characteristics is much more related to their classroom behavior (learning included) than one can imagine. If students perceive and believe teachers are concerned about their individual learning, then their attitude towards accepting or learning what is being taught appears to be more instinctively motivated, or more positively influenced, which leads one to believe their level of learning will be greater. On the other hand, if a teacher is extremely effective in delivering the information being taught, but the students' perception of the teacher is threatening or impersonal, then the level of learning is decreased from what it could and/or should be.

The influence of the teacher's "personal commitment to their individual learning," *as perceived and believed by students*, is probably the most learning related motivational factor in the classroom. This is overlooked and yet a significant factor relating to student learning. It is something very difficult to be taught for a

Chapter 3: Teaching Methodologies

teacher to do. It appears almost intrinsic to the character, personality, persona, and commitment of the person teaching. Excellent teachers have it! Maybe that is why many excellent teachers often appear to do their job in spite of financial related issues—they love their job responsibility (student learning) and the students know, believe, and are motivated to learn because of it. This characteristic of excellent teachers is so common and would be difficult to be taught by any teacher education programs. Excellent teachers have it; others have to work harder to try to display/achieve it. Students, as well as others, react to what they see, feel, and hear! *Sound familiar?*

Now the more teachers can do, the "improvements" teachers have to make, and to assure these types of teachers are the greater majority employed, is the subject of this book. It is not so much how excellent teachers are identified but the changes that have to be implemented to identify less effective teachers, then improve them, all to significantly increase "student learning."

IMPROVEMENTS: ENSURE LEARNING

- ▶ Ethically incorporate all three receptive learning modes for teaching all course measurable objectives.
- ▶ Create genuine student interest in all course objectives and abolish threats of failure or threats of any kind.
- ▶ Create intermittent course tests to measure student learning and evaluate teaching effectiveness of all major course objectives. Utilize the results for the improvement of instruction methodologies and re-teaching.

- Display a recognizable classroom attitude and demeanor that the teacher's primary priority is "student learning."

Chapter 4: Teacher Preparation

Preparation is the most important step in teaching. If preparation is inadequate the results will certainly be poor levels of learning characterized by a number of disruptive classroom factors. Poor preparation leads to poor control of the class and poor student learning.

The Learning Plan

In the world of education the emphasis is on teaching—expecting students to learn the way the teacher teaches; emphasizing the verbal learning mode when teaching.

In the real world the emphasis is on learning—expecting teachers to teach the way the students learn; emphasizing multi-learning modes when teaching.

Successful people plan their work—then work their plan! So, to teach effectively in and for the real world necessitates the pre- preparation and development of a "Learning Plan." This plan, *concentrating specifically on ensuring student learning*, consists of the Topic Objective, Methods of Instruction, Analysis of Learning, and Improvement. This Plan is essential to initiate and continuously improve student learning—and is described as follows:

TOPIC OBJECTIVES

The first step in preparation is to divide the course or lesson information into topic objectives. The most important information to be learned must be represented by stated/written objectives—the reason for teaching the topic or whatever. Call it what whatever: objectives, results, aims, purposes, reasons, etc.—the knowledge to be learned must be represented by a statement describing the resulting expectations of what is being taught, and *to be learned*. The purpose for doing it!

Example: "At the end of this (lesson, session, topic, etc.) the student will be able to correctly (perform, complete, compute, solve, etc.)…"

Example: "As a result of this… the student will be able to accurately interpret the author's meanings…"

Example: "At the end of this… the student will be able to correctly solve a problem containing …"

Example: "As a result of this… the student will be able to both accurately investigate and verbally communicate the…"

Note: These examples state the objective of your teaching—what the student will be able to know, perform, etc. as a result of the teaching effort. It is the necessary basis for the remaining preparation including: Methods of Instruction, Analysis of Learning, and Improvement. It is the most important step in preparation of teaching any subject matter. It is the necessary starting point.

Now, the entire course or body of knowledge that the teacher is responsible for will have to be represented by these objectives. This means thoroughly pre-reviewing the course or lesson content and writing the objectives. When written, the objectives represent the initial pre-planned stepped blueprint of the course—all necessary to ensure the planning, implementation, and analysis of student learning. (How can a teacher analyze the level of student learning if they don't know what the students were supposed to have learned?) *Without Topic Objectives, teaching to ensure learning and subsequent continuous improvement will be next to impossible to document and achieve.* Therefore, each objective should be recorded as the first statement in the teacher's one page "Learning Plan"—that is the written/formatted outline for that particular teaching session (the course will be made up of cumulative Learning Plans). In reality the Learning Plan is a comprehensive one page document per objective and is a necessary teaching/learning working transcript. It details what is to be learned, how to teach it, an analysis of learning, and improvements! It is the teacher's essential guide to ensure student learning and continuous improvement. *So now, the first essential statement in the Learning Plan is the Topic Objective.*

Note that the lesson material itself (actual information to be taught and learned) is separate from the Learning Plan and can take traditional forms such as text books, notes, documents, etc., from which the objectives are derived.

METHODS OF INSTRUCTION

It is the preparation of the Methods of Instruction that will determine how well the students receive the information presented. Remember that individuals receive and process information via three traditional modes: Hearing, Seeing, and Feeling. If a teacher decides to only verbally teach then they are only reaching those biased to hearing, leaving out those receptive otherwise. **To be on the receptive wavelength of all the students, teachers must present the information utilizing the three modes.** To do this requires that the one most familiar with the subject matter, the teacher, develop strategies to accomplish this. What is it that the teacher can *ethically* invent, develop, present, involve students in, etc. that compels the student to not only hear, but to see and physically experience the subject matter effects of the topic being taught. "Seeing," of course, would involve utilizing experiences from various traditional media methods—to real life visual applications. Receiving information through "Feeling" involves experiencing physical involvement, reactions, applications, movement, etc. Examples of teaching methodologies involving all the modes of learning are around us in everyday life. One only has to ethically relate similar processes to the classroom. Whether a student is to learn a mathematical formula, chemical procedure, geographical term, language grammar, philosophical concept,

Chapter 4: Teacher Preparation

poetry, etc.—seeing the results of the topic objective applied, in addition to physically utilizing/applying it, is essential to ensure learning.

One glaring example/revelation is in teaching the non-visual internal structure of a material—an abstract/theoretical subject. The preach-teach scenario was to draw the molecular structure on the white board and verbally describe the physical results from changes in/to the structure. Student testing always produced mixed levels of results. As part of analyzing the test grades, versus the topic objective, improvement in the teaching methodology was obvious and necessary in order to improve student learning. Thus a real-life demonstration of the actual effects of the molecular change in the material was developed and every time that real-life demonstration was performed (to a class of 35 to 45 students) some student always yelled out appreciatively: "that's what my chemistry teacher meant!" Ironically, many teachers were taught the same concept verbally and never really understood the concept until they experienced it in real life applications. Seeing the application of a concept is believing! The methodology was also extended by having students investigate examples of the concept application outside of the classroom and report back their findings. This represented the "Feeling" mode of learning and was verified by almost always 100 percent level of learning response to the class testing of that topic objective. A significant improvement from prior learning of that objective.

The Methods of Instruction developed by a teacher will be unique to each person teaching the topic assigned. A teacher's experience, knowledge, demeanor, and tone may dictate the way this is done. It must be developed for each objective, recorded as part of the learning plan, and continuously improved through analysis of the student's level of learning versus the related method of instruction. Again, this is a necessary part of the Learning Plan and is the part most essential to improvement. *So, now the Learning Plan has two essentials: the Topic Objective and the Methods of Instruction.*

ANALYSIS OF LEARNING

Testing: To get to the point where you are reading this text one must realize that you have had experience in testing. If not as a teacher; certainly as a student. Therefore most readers are familiar with written essay, computer formats, multiple choice, and practical applications—as they are the most common experiences of the education survivor. An example: Everybody sitting and responding by computer to multiple questions of preach teaching is the very nature of testing verbal learning. Good for verbal learners—others, not so good! Effective teachers have found that there are many other methods of determining the levels of learning—some actually involve learning while testing. As an example: Giving portions of questions to small groups of students, made up from a large class, with the goal of having each small group work to verbally agree on answers to their assigned questions. Then, have each group present their answers verbally in the large class meeting until all groups were heard and involved in the derivation of those answers. Then, after that learning experience—traditionally test for the level of learning of the Topic Objective.

The important point in testing is to determine how well (at what level) all the students learned the material from the Methods of Instruction, and then use that data to improve the Methods of Instruction.

Analyzing Learning: The traditionally accepted graphical analysis of class grades is a Bell shape curve ranging from effective learning—high scores to non-effective learning—low scores. It is obvious to ensure learning of **all** students in the class that a curved graph and/or low scores indicates an immediate and necessary change in the Methods of Instruction—even to the point of re-teaching the Topic Objective.

A teacher's goal depicting student learning should be a high range of grades, with minimal dispersion, representing the successful level of learning of that respective Objective for all students in the class.

It is apparent that levels of learning, naturally due to variances in students, will change with each different class/group, even when utilizing the same methods of instruction. This is reason enough to continually improve the teaching methodologies based on an Analysis of Learning of each Topic Objective. The real challenge of the teacher is not to try to change the students but to change the Methods of Instruction which in turn will change the learning outcome of the students.

Now, even with the variance in student groups it seems reasonable to accept the concept that learning will improve with most teaching methodology improvements. This is readily apparent from analyzing grades, resulting from improvements in teaching methodologies (for individual Topic Objectives), evolved over many classes. To make improvements one time, based on student's levels of learning, is defeating the goal of continuous improvement and depriving the learners of the teacher's professional abilities. That is why this should be an on-going process, analyzing the test results of student learning of the corresponding Topic Objective and then improving the Methods of Instruction. This is not a one-time event but rather a continual process of improvement. This analysis and improvement should occur every time an individual Topic Objective teaching/learning process is implemented (each time it is taught). If you are teaching to ensure learning you must analyze the learning and improve the Methods of Instruction continuously. That is how a teacher becomes excellent at what they do. Without a continuous process of improvement natural complacency appears and student learning suffers the consequences that we as a nation currently exhibit: mediocre international ranking, low college admissions SAT scores, high drop-out rates, and disenchanted stay-outs.

So, now, the Learning Plan has three essentials: the Topic Objective, Methods of Instruction, and an Analysis of Learning.

IMPROVEMENT

The real challenge of the teacher is not to try to change the students, but to improve the Methods of Instruction, which in turn will improve the level of learning of the students. This is the real-world proven concept of analysis and continuous improvement and appears to be standard practice for those perceived as "excellent" teachers.

Realistic examples of needed improvement are apparent when a topic objective is taught utilizing the verbal methodology only. Testing usually reveals who the better verbal learners are, and those who are not—the grades achieved will make these distinctions readily apparent. *Improving the teaching methodology, utilizing the multi-modes of hearing, seeing, and feeling, will typically result in quite different learning and grading results. Instead of the grades being skewed in favor of the more natural verbal learners, the grades tend to portray a more uniform and higher level of student learning for all*—**Students learn easier and thus better.** Analysis of student learning resulting from the Methods of Instruction (as described in the learning plan) tells the teacher how effective the teaching methodology was and thus is documented justification for planning and stating new improvements.

Another realistic reason to document "Methods of Instruction" improvement is related to one's teaching performance evaluation. "Learning Plans" are documented examples of improvement and can serve to positively justify reappointment and/or continued employment. It not only says that "I am doing my job," but documents credible effort to continuously improve student learning—the most important responsibility of the teacher. It is hard to imagine a supervisor, school district, school board, parents, etc. not positively accepting the very nature of documented improvement—especially when evident and directly relative to improvement in student learning. One often hears the statement that the best job insurance is: "make yourself so valuable to your employer that they cannot afford to be without you." Under normal circumstances it is difficult to imagine an educational organization divesting itself of well documented "effective" teachers. Learning Plans are an excellent investment in improving student learning as well as documenting professional performance. The very nature of successful improvement is derived from the well proven axiom: "Plan your work first, then work your plan."

So now, the complete Learning Plan has four essentials: the Topic Objective, Instruction Methods, Analysis of Learning, and Improvement.

The Learning Plan, a working document, is the teacher's guide to ensure and continuously improve student learning.

A THOUGHT

For too many years teachers have been focusing on just verbal "Teaching"—taking learning for granted, even when deceptively justified. Now, due to our mediocre international ranking in education, low college admissions SAT scores, high drop-out rates, and an indeterminable number of disenchanted stay-outs; it's time to significantly improve what is being done. **Now is the time to re-direct the focus to "Learning" and let the process of "how students learn" dictate "how teachers teach"—instead of the other way around.**

In the *world of education* the emphasis is on "Teaching," expecting students to learn from the way the teacher teaches—emphasizing lesson plans, a single mode of learning (hearing) through verbal lecture, and reward/penalty grading. In the *real world* emphasis is on "Learning," expecting teachers to teach the way students learn—emphasizing learning plans, multi-learning mode teaching, with analysis of learning and continuous improvement. Professional educators have a responsibility to demonstrate their response to the rhetorical question: *What bottom line benefits the educational consumer (the learner)* **the most:** *Teaching or Learning?*

IMPROVEMENTS: TEACHER PREPARATION

- Divide all major course information into measureable Topic Objectives.
- Determine multi-mode Methods of Instruction for each Topic Objective.
- Analyze learning (the range and dispersion of test grades) for all Topic Objectives
- Improve the Methods of Instruction based on the Analysis of Learning
- Create a one-page Learning Plan for each Topic Objective stating: the Topic Objective, Methods of Instruction, Analysis of Learning, and Improvements.
- Amend the Learning Plan sections: "Analysis of Learning" and "Improvement"—on a continuous basis, each time a Topic Objective is taught.

Chapter 5: Teacher Evaluation

The Process

As part of the process of improving teaching and learning instructional managers must analyze: How teachers are currently evaluated and How teachers should be evaluated.

How are teachers currently evaluated? The prevailing processes in education are far removed from evaluating teaching performance significantly based on student learning. First, most learning institutions and school districts have their own faculty evaluation systems drafted and redrafted until approval is reached among faculty organizations, unions, administration, etc. The result is that they are very "diverse" in order to gain the approval of all constituent groups, therefore, a variety of categories make up the evaluation.

The contents of an evaluation can typically include: *First*, a peer evaluation whereby a peer faculty member observes classroom presentations and writes a report; *Second,* an administrative observation of classroom performance where an administrator observes classroom performance and reports—usually once/twice a semester, announced and/or unannounced according to the faculty agreement for that institution/district; *Third,* a student evaluation of faculty which typically reflects the student's perception of the faculty member; and *Fourth,* a faculty member's self-report of activities, etc. All the evaluation items are generally put together and then reviewed between the faculty member and their supervisor and/or a committee made up of reviewers. The current process is certainly comprehensive; utilizing all parties concerned, but the real and most important focus of what the evaluation should be is too often minimized. **A faculty evaluation, specifically relating to the teacher's foremost job responsibility, must reveal the level of classroom student learning achieved; all documented by testing based on comprehensive measurable objectives of the course.** This is basic to implementing the practice of "continuous improvement."

In current practice it is rare to find overall classroom learning documented per specific objectives and then analyzed as part of a faculty member's performance evaluation, let alone being used as a basis for improvement. The logical outcome of teaching is *student learning* and that should be the basis for faulty evaluation. So, how was this logical and most important faculty responsibility ignored? It appears this primary responsibility has been increasingly diminished over time by layered administrative systems in which the need to follow complex procedures impedes logical and effective reasoning. Thus school systems were able to shift the accountability for classroom outcomes to the consumer (the student). They were and are successful at doing this because most parents, consumers, or whoever feel inadequate to disagree. *The public's ingrained perception of a teacher appears to be not to question them or the principal, and to stay out of the principal's office!* Who, as a consumer, has the nerve to ask the teacher to show their effectiveness ranking documented by student class grades? Students resist asking because they perceive the teacher may retaliate against them. Parents resist because they perceive the teacher may retaliate against their children. Asking the principal or instructional supervisor usually winds up in the standard answer, "We already have a comprehensive evaluation system." *Note: As the public demand for accountability increases someone eventually will communicate to teachers, administrators, and school boards and insist to be shown the level of student learning and resultant level of teaching effectiveness taking place in the classrooms. It can be documented specifically by computing a class grade average based on a comprehensive final examination or cumulative test grades; representing the student level of achievement of the course objectives.* Paying consumers feel it is only logical that one should be able to see what is received for the money. Unfortunately too many schools would be confounded in that they would not know where to begin—no records of tests/exams tied to specific and comprehensive course objectives, teacher performance related to student learning non-existent, thus teacher effectiveness ratings not available. Although, somewhere and sometime, someone in our nation's school districts is actually reviewing documented student learning and relating it to faculty evaluation and that is a great step forward, but that process itself is few and far between and appears nonexistent—Educators and the public must applaud anyone doing it.

Problematic Example: A faculty review session where all the parties gave their input and a reviewer in the group, who was appointed by a new rule asking for input from outside the normal faculty members group, stood up and said (paraphrased), "This is a total joke. This faculty member is not doing the job and should require serious improvement but you people are afraid to do anything because you have to work with him/her and you are scared of the unions/legal/personal repercussions." He was upset and stalked out of the review disgusted. Needless to say, the faculty member being reviewed had problems but because of the review process (which subsequently supported and applauded his/her performance) he/she continued to repeat as "the only failure in the classroom." Imagine the student learning that was neglected, year after year, because of a system that never entertained the idea of reviewing what and how the students learned from this teacher. How can a diverse nation be a leader in education when schools and colleges do not analyze, and make continual instructional improvements based on how well the students learn from their teacher? *It is only logical to evaluate a teacher on their documented instruction, improvement, and how well their students learn.* Schools and colleges do not appear to be doing this and this must be changed!

How should teachers be evaluated? It is more than obvious the lack of teachers being evaluated based on the level of learning of their students is a major part of the education dilemma in the

United States. That is how schools and colleges unwittingly promote poor teaching and subsequent poorer learning. How many jobs/professions are there where the persons paid to perform a task are not evaluated on the outcome of that task? Very few! Even politicians are reviewed on the effects of their performance, at the voting booth. Look at the professions of sales, entertainment, construction, transportation, etc. Persons performing tasks are evaluated on the outcome of those tasks. That is how whatever is produced is improved! Note: The end of the Second World War brought about a manufacturing revolution in Japan. After the war the products produced in Japan were commonly referred to as junk! People purposely looked for the signature quotation, "Made in USA," before they purchased, otherwise they were taking a chance on buying a product that would fall apart or fail. Then, thanks to an American statistician, Dr. Edwards Deming, Japanese manufacturing adopted an improvement process. In general, they documented what they produced, analyzed that documentation, and then made subsequent improvements. They repeated this process "continuously" and thus significantly improved the products they made. Their reformation from producing junk to producing some of the best products in the world is common knowledge and is an example of what can be accomplished through objective evaluation of productivity. Is this comparing apples to oranges: manufacturing to teaching? You miss the point if you think that! This is reinforcing the logical concept that to significantly improve what you produce, you must *continuously*: document what you produce, analyze it, and then improve it. Now, what do teachers produce? The result of the teaching process is the learning by the student. That is the product of what teachers produce—student learning! Some teacher organizations, government studies, accreditation agencies, etc. can and do produce rhetoric that unwittingly fogs and/or expands the basic responsibility of the teacher. So much so that the initial and foremost responsibility of the teacher, "student learning," is minimized. In reality, no matter what protective groups relate about a teacher's responsibility, the bottom line to the public consumer and/or parent is, "What learning took place?" It only makes sense; in current practice the consumers pay the teacher to teach a class, the teacher teaches and no one knows what overall level of learning took place in the class. Yes, grades are given to individual students, but where are all the final examination grades, reflecting the achievement of the course objectives, made available? They document the teaching effectiveness and resultant level of learning that took place in the class. Alternatively, the teacher has a record of all the final *course* grades given however even that record, notoriously erroneous to verifiable student learning is certainly not a primary and/or credible basis for teacher evaluation.

Now, somewhere, sometime, evaluation based on verifiable student learning might take place, but it does not appear to be common place. First, to document what the students have learned, and the effectiveness of the teacher, it is necessary to test the student's knowledge and/or performance of course objectives. How can any process be improved, teaching included, unless what is produced is documented, analyzed, and then used as a basis for determining improvement. Again, the problem is that too many teachers are not evaluated on the learning of their students. In fact, most evaluation systems of faculty are far removed from any documented learning that took place in their class. The most common reviewed is the "Student Evaluation of Faculty" survey that focuses on the student's perception of their teacher. This is far removed from documenting the level of learning that took place in the class. The learning that takes place in the class has to be the prime focus of the teacher and the level of learning should serve as the documented basis of teacher performance. This information must then be used in teaching improvement planning and faculty appointment decision making. To be a world leader in education it is necessary to have the best teachers. That is, teachers who are able to promote the highest level of student learning given the objectives of their course and documented by formal and comprehensive testing.

Education has to focus on "student learning." If educators focus on "student learning," then the teaching that takes place in and to different groups (socioeconomic, urban, rural, etc.) will have to be varied and different to elicit the highest level of learning from those individual and varied groups of learners. Different methods for different groups! The converse is obvious: If teachers continue to preach-teach, similar to all groups, then they will receive what they produce; higher levels of learning from those students/groups who adapt to preach-teach and varying failure from those that do not. The effect of this is a matter of a mediocre ranking and must be changed. One shoe size does not fit all and that must be the challenge of the teacher, to elicit the highest level of learning from different groups by utilizing different teaching methodologies for different groups.

An exemplary teacher, called Dr. Ed, said his biggest challenge was teaching math to a group of immigrants whose country of origin lacked formal education. He said he gave up on the classroom format for this group and took them outside on the rear school lawn and, using the required math course concepts, related those concepts to crop planting processes (something they could relate to because of their agricultural background) to teach the objectives of the course. Yes, they grew crops, learned math, and met the objectives of the course. Dr. Ed was elated the level of learning was so high in a group that no other teacher wanted to even begin to teach. Now, imagine the pre-planning Dr. Ed had to do to relate the learning environment (methods of instruction) to the objectives of the course and the difficult background of the students. Dr. Ed truly believed the only failure in the classroom was the teacher —he is genuinely missed. Thanks, Dr. Ed!

To improve student learning there should be an expectation that instructional supervisors require documentation and analysis of how course topic objectives relate to corresponding examination/test grades, in each teacher's course. The graphical representation of those grades versus objectives would present immediate recognition of teaching methods, where necessary, that need to be improved. That should be the major part of the teacher's continuous improvement plan. Also, the faculty member's class grade average based on a comprehensive final examination or cumulative tests, for all enrolled students, could/should be analyzed. This would document the student level of learning and the teaching effectiveness. The public perception is that they are paying for learning and currently cannot even find out how much, or how well, learning took place. It is not a convincing argument to the public/students that they should only know their own, or their own children's scores. The teacher's primary responsibility is for student learning and the teacher teaches a class, so what student learning took place in the class? **It must be known in order to evaluate and improve.** It also serves as a motivation tool to focus on student learning instead of verbal lecture teaching. It is time to reverse the roles and give the public/consumer the information to evaluate what they purchase. The bottom line is to modify the system's philosophical focus from lecture-teaching to documented "student learning," and then we will be on the road to significantly "Improving Teaching and Learning in Schools and Colleges."

A Thought

A parent is concerned because their child received a low grade in a course at school and approaches the teacher for an explanation. After a typical conversation the parent walks away convinced the low grade is well deserved and probably feels guilty they are part of the cause.

On the other hand, it *would be beneficial to both parties* if the teacher could show the parent the corresponding grades of all the other students (names omitted) and how those grades compare to their child's grades relative to each specific course objective measured. This would specifically document deficient areas and justify discussion regarding future improvement—problem solving instead of laying blame. Also, is this the only student in the class who received a low grade? If so, the parents could understand and accept that there is merit to the teacher's reasoning. Additionally if the teacher documents his/her effectiveness rating for this class in comparison to the school's minimum acceptable level of student learning for a class (a class graded average based on a comprehensive final exam or cumulative test grades) it would lend credibility to the teacher's verification of the low grade in question. Again, if the teacher would show the class examination grades (names omitted) then it would document if the low learning level of the student in question is isolated or a trend and thus verify the effectiveness of the methods of instruction. This, in turn would enlighten the parents, would lend itself to documented credibility and diminish alienating the education consumer.

Most excellent teachers have no problem documenting their effectiveness and generally will when discussing grade problems with parents or students. The converse usually holds true and therein lies the problem! The public's view is that they are an educational consumer in the "real world" and therefore apply the common reasoning that it is best to "check the depth of the water before diving into the pool." If prior student learning documentation and resultant teacher effectiveness ratings do not exist, then education decision making to the public/consumer is just a gamble. This will have to change in order to significantly and continuously improve teaching and learning, as well as meet consumer demands in and for the "real world!"

IMPROVEMENTS: TEACHER EVALUATION

- Document measurable course objectives for all major course topics taught.

- Document comprehensive final examinations and cumulative tests that include all major course measurable objectives, for all courses taught.

- Document a "class grade average for each assigned course, grading the class level of learning and resultant teaching effectiveness.

- Compute the "class grade average" using the comprehensive final examination grades or cumulative test grades: all enrolled students, no exemptions.

- Prepare a continuous teaching improvement plan by analyzing the range and dispersion of test grades for individual topic objectives—versus the methods of instruction.

- Demonstrate re-appointment based on acceptable class grade averages in the most recent classes, and an acceptable continuous teaching improvement plan.

Chapter 6: Teacher Contracts

Types and Content

To improve teaching and learning, schools and colleges must analyze the effects of current teacher contracts and then revise them to specifically state job responsibility requirements.

Teacher contracts should be subject to the *job responsibility* of producing an acceptable level of *student learning*, and unfortunately they do not appear to do that. Note that the legal contents of teacher contracts will vary from state to state but the outcome of awarding a contract, and how that directly affects student learning, is what is most important. Remember, the public educational institution is, or should be, in business for one reason only: *student learning!*

Typically, there are two types of full-time faculty teaching contracts used in public education:

First: Probationary Contract. This is written for faculty who have not completed a probationary period, but are employed in a tenure granting position; better described as a "tenure track" appointment. Generally, probation periods for tenure track faculty vary from two to seven years, depending on the particular school, school district, college, and/or university.

Probationary faculty should be, and generally are, subject to administrative review of their performance prior to awarding every new annual probationary contract. The school administration usually has the right to not renew a probationary contract without showing cause. In other words, they do not have to give a reason for not renewing a contract and can terminate the faculty employment whenever and for whatever they choose. However, this is not always the case in a probationary appointment, as a faculty member in say the 5th or 6th year of a 7-year tenure granting position has gained legal support in some states for requiring the institution to show cause, even though they are not legally bound to. The reasoning for this is if the institution has employed them for four years or so without documented problems, meaning their performance was acceptable, they should be given a chance to correct any deficiencies cited before the tenure decision. Therefore, the early years in the probationary appointment are now being focused on more intently. Also, once the faculty member has completed the probationary process and is tenured (tenure decisions vary among institutions from somewhat automatic to exceedingly selective) it is the school's responsibility to show cause for non-contract renewal. *This process, as discussed further in this chapter, can be, and generally is, a huge and significant impediment to student learning.*

Second: Tenured Faculty Continuing Contract. This is an automatic contract awarded annually and continuously.

Note: It is important that critics of education understand and acknowledge that the strong majority of tenured faculty are very professional and excel in their academic responsibilities. The problems related to tenure tend to only occur with a small amount of tenured faculty but take up an enormous amount of administrative time, legal proceedings, and create significant dissention and distraction—all contrary to student learning. Thus the negative public perception and notoriety of the term—"Tenure."

In explanation: More often than not, the legal process of a non-acceptable tenured faculty performance issue is so involved and time delaying that most schools avoid it. In effect, the most often occurring way a tenured faculty member is terminated is when the faculty member commits a felony, then they are placed on administrative leave pending the outcome of the judicial process. If convicted of the felony, they are usually terminated. If not convicted the tenured faculty member generally resumes their school duties. Any non-acceptable performance, other than the commission of a felony, is disputable and winds up in lengthy review between the tenured faculty member and the school administration. Again, more often than not, this process takes years to work through given that the school must provide remedial education and/or training for the tenured faculty member based on the deliberated concept that the faculty member's performance during the probation period was acceptable, and because it is not acceptable now, must be the responsibility of the school. Thus the school must provide remedial education and/or training to bring the poor performance back from deficient to acceptable.

Here is the problem: All the time the remedial education and/or retraining continues the student classes continue, semester after semester, with the ineffective faculty performance tending to repeat until improved. Even if the courses taught by the faculty member could be staffed by someone else, which is generally not the case because there are just not enough faculty to cover extra contingencies/areas of expertise like this, the faculty member in question could and most likely would file a formal grievance against his/her replacement and could be returned to the classroom pending the outcome of the grievance and the retraining. Exceptions to this include assigning the faculty member in question non-questionable duties for the review/repair period at a double cost to the school (replacement plus faculty member salary in question).

Ineffective performance of tenured teachers, specifically when documented by low levels of student learning, is immeasurable! This includes not only poor classroom teaching and/or student learning but more importantly: *resistance to course and program revisions, incorporating new technology, and other curriculum changes advised by external advisory groups and/or school administration.* Resistance to such changes, and in many cases just outright refusal, results in promoting student learning obsolescence along with the start of a lengthy legal show cause complaint against the faculty member. This legal process usually winds up causing polarization of faculty supporters/non-supporters which increases internally due to the lengthy duration of the legal proceedings, and many times the end result appears to be

CHAPTER 6: TEACHER CONTRACTS

worse than the initial problem itself, even though it is not because the ultimate loser is the student. That is one of the major reasons school administrations, more often than not, do not pursue specific and necessary staffing changes. Again, legal avoidance of tenured faculty deficient performance only promotes and eventually leads to obsolescence, the direct opposite of the concept of continuous improvement. Currently teacher tenure, **in the case of just a few faculty**, is a contractual situation that hinders school administration from acting, let alone acting quickly, to resolve deficient performance that is an impediment to student learning.

Here are some of the foremost and justifiable arguments in favor of tenure:

- *Protection from being fired for personal, political, or similar reasons.*
- *Stops schools from replacing high cost teachers with low cost new teachers.*
- *Protects teachers for teaching controversial topics.*
- *Promises a secure profession.*
- *A reward for positive and continuous prior teaching evaluations.*
- *Protects faculty by lay-off related to and by seniority.*

This list continues with additional and "sensible" reasons why proven teachers should have some protection as a group. *Ironically there appears to be no relationship to documented student learning and continuous improvement in the tenure arguments/reasons and that is, and if not should be, the primary job responsibility of the Teacher.* In contrast: There are very few people in the "real world" who have employment, a job, or profession that strongly and legally protects them from being replaced except for the commission of a felony. Even a self-employed person has to answer to their customers for what they produce! It does not make sense to promote poor teaching by guaranteeing continuing employment of underperforming teachers. Teacher representative groups will say this is not true, there is a process for resolving poor teaching problems. Yes, but in reality the process may take years if it is successful, is riddled with legal proceedings, is a major institutional morale distraction with monumental documentation and reviews, and generally winds up with the students, semester after semester until resolved, suffering the most. It is a process operationally ineffective to resolve teacher problems, creates more problems, and then amplifies them. Currently "Tenure" appears to benefit teacher's job longevity, certainly has recognizable value for students, but is lacking accountability in its current design. **Therefore, continuous teacher contracts (Tenure) should be subject to documented performance of the teacher's job responsibility; producing an acceptable level of student learning and continuous improvement.** This is a reasonable expectation.

If the students are not learning at an acceptable level then require teaching improvement planning, and implementation. Not doing this is almost criminal in nature, knowing deficient teaching resulting in negative student learning is taking place. Remember, students move on, semester to semester, and build on the prior learning accomplished. If learning in a particular semester was significantly poor, they are at an extreme disadvantage in the forthcoming class. Unfortunately, awareness and action to halt this type of detrimental damage is typically overlooked when evaluating faculty and renewing contracts, significantly so when the teacher is job protected by tenure. Documented student learning, when below an acceptable level, and the subsequent negative effects, are rarely factors conditional in tenured faculty reappointment. *Is the teacher's job conditional on the learning of the students? No! Should it be? Yes!* The public's strong perception is that if they are paying the costs of education (taxes and/or tuition or both) then it certainly makes sense it should be. Proponents of tenure argue teachers are well evaluated by students, other faculty, and administration and all of these are taken into account in the appointment process. This type of evaluation process is the nature of the problem! "Student Evaluation of Faculty" (SEF's) do not document student learning. They are only the student's perception of the faculty member *before the final grade is given!* The relationship between a favorable student perception of the teacher and documented testing/learning of approved course objectives can, and possibly will be, quite different. At times tenured faculty lament they had great students in *the* class (in reverse the students had a great perception of the teacher) but the students were just too slow to learn and specific course material was left out. There was no documented course objectives testing to uncover the lack of teaching/learning, the teacher received high evaluation scores, and the students moved on lacking what they should have known. As a result, the tenured faculty member moves on to engage a new class with similar deficient performance, and a new contract year with the same old problem. Class after class and somewhere down the line the student faces the fact they have a problem and must accelerate their learning to catch up what they have missed, or just say it is now too difficult and drop out. All of this down the line is directly related back to poor learning in a prior class and is allowed to continue because of operationally guaranteed employment. Unfortunately the current tenure process guarantees, *for just a few faculty,* the perpetuation of deficient teacher performance resulting in poor student learning and is just another one of the major root causes of a failing educational system. Remember, many states do have a show cause requirement for non-reappointment of faculty however traditional "union/faculty association bargained contracts" just make the "show cause" process more difficult because the contractual job responsibility of attaining an acceptable level of *documented* student learning and continuous improvement is not a requirement for reappointment. It is reasonable to contend that the more difficult it is to be accountable for documented student learning and improvement the poorer the education outcomes for students will be in that system: district/unit/school/college.

So What Has To Be Done? *Directly relate teacher re-appointment contracts to documented student learning and continuous improvement.* That way the school would be reappointing effective teachers, in that their students learn and document their learning through approved course objectives and resultant testing. The opponents argue that the teacher's job is just not teaching! That not only implies but actually is the reason student learning is seriously subjugated or overlooked as the paramount teaching job responsibility and is the nature of the overall problem. Many teachers contend because their job may include meetings, paid retraining, coaching, counseling, study groups, professional organizations, etc., that faculty must have a spread out evaluation focusing on all their duties. This usually winds up in a pro-rated evaluation process that obliterates and/or minimizes "student learning" to a non-accountable, *and in most cases non-existent,* weight of performance. The current teacher evaluation process is generally accepted as "comprehensive" and is a designated pro-rated review process including peer review, administrative review, student evaluation of faculty (SEF's) professional involvements, etc. Unfortunately, *the whole concept of documenting what and how well the students have learned appears to be minimized.* To make matters more diffused, the actual documentation of what and how well the students learned is either not available, ignored, or subjugated to a laundry list of the other so called priority items, agreed upon by a bargaining unit or a committee. **Instructional supervisors find it very rare to be involved in a faculty evaluation that compares collective student class grades to comprehensive course objectives for the purpose of instructional analysis and continuous improvement.** How such a basic job responsibility is minimized is a tribute to years of evolving evaluation practices that tend to emphasize everything but documented student learning.

Unfortunately, the current faculty evaluation process leads to school praise of some faculty members who have questionable performance in a classroom, and actually reinforces their questionable performance. It actually makes it harder to implement improvement because of this type of erroneous evaluation.

Make "teacher contracts" subject to documented student learning and continuous improvement. Even at that rate the satisfactory amount or level of student learning will be verbalized, and in itself, will constitute major discussion. At least the appointment of teachers to classes will be based on what and how the student's learn from that teacher. This is the way it should be in the *real world* and not concealed by a list of other so-called priority responsibilities. There is no greater teacher priority or responsibility than of what and how well the students learn in the classroom. That is the bottom line and should be the only *significant* basis for reappointment. Anything less just degrades accountability and degrades the teaching effectiveness of the school and the education system it represents. Critics of public education perceive that the present system is an excellent example of what happens when poor learning, predicated on ineffective teaching, is allowed to take place. Think of the improvement it would make if teachers were appointed on how well their students learned the documented material they are responsible for. Student's final examination grades or cumulative tests, reflecting the level of learning of all course objectives and resultant teaching effectiveness, would tell the whole story. Anything else is just camouflage, and an injustice to the customer/consumer—the student!

A Thought

About Tenure: This is a controversial topic debated endlessly by critics and supporters. Critics are generally those who have to deal with the detriments of Tenure whereas supporters are generally those who work in the system and see it as protection against unfair treatment. The arguments against Tenure are usually generated by those having to deal with a small group of problematic faculty; a situation which in turn affects the entire school, including student learning. *It appears reasonable that the solution to the Tenure issue must be made in the best interest of school's purpose—student learning; thus it seems logical to make changes to resolve the problems relative to improving the small groups of problematic faulty and yet retain the fundamentals of Tenure—job protection.*

In Explanation: It appears that the major amount of tenured faculty at an institution of learning are proven teachers dedicated to their profession and make reasonable efforts to work with administration to resolve problems and stay current in their individual fields of study. The problems that do occur generally occur with a small minority of the faculty, which unfortunately take up to 90 percent of inconsequential managerial and legal time. During this time consuming process, the collateral damage inflicted within the school too many times becomes intolerable. People become alienated, faculty and staff take sides, others become involved in issues because of friendships and involve parents, students, and/or board members, etc. Therefore, the efforts to improve student learning by replacing or improving a faculty member who's performance is persistently deficient but is tenured is most generally avoided. To fix this problem we need to revise continuous teacher contracts that currently have minimal evaluative connection to the job responsibility of student learning. They should be replaced **with continuing type contracts** *specifically subject to tenured faculty demonstrating an acceptable level of teacher effectiveness (student learning)* documented by computing class grade averages. This type of contractual employment is much more in keeping with the *real world* concept of accountability.

Improving Tenure contracts by requiring documentation of acceptable levels of student learning and continuous improvement when necessary would remove the public stigma surrounding this contractual status and reinforce a perception of teacher excellence. It would also support the necessity and requirement of immediate improvement for tenured faculty who have deficiencies. This type of contract would ensure student learning and promote a more positive public and consumer perception of education.

IMPROVEMENTS: TEACHER CONTRACTS

- Identify all courses the teacher is assigned to teach.
- Require preparation of measurable objectives for all major topics in each course assigned.
- Require comprehensive final course examinations that include all major course measurable objectives, for all students enrolled in all courses assigned, no exemptions.
- Document a "class grade average," grading the level of learning of all course measureable objectives and resultant teaching effectiveness, for each assigned course.
- Compute the "class grade average," using comprehensive final examination grades or cumulative test grades; all enrolled students, no exemptions.
- Demonstrate an acceptable level of teaching effectiveness based on the most recent "class grade averages."
- Prepare a continuous improvement teaching plan by analyzing the range and dispersion of test grades for

individual topic objectives—versus the methods of instruction.

- Receive, for contract reappointment, approval of all aforementioned requirements.

Chapter 7: Teacher Education

Programs and Learning

Improvement in teaching and learning must be one of the resultant products of the teacher education system/process in the United States.

In practice, *most* teachers in the elementary and secondary (High School) systems are minimally required to have a bachelor's degree and a teaching certificate, usually issued by the teacher's individual state. The teaching certification process generally requires the completion of a specific number and type of teacher education, general education, and major area of study courses. Whereas, faculty/professors at the community college, 4-year college, and university systems have individual higher degree requirements but, for the most part, **do not** require teacher education courses, including "how to teach."

Traditionally the faculty/professors at the community college level have masters degrees and significant job experience in the subjects they are teaching versus the faculty/professors at the college/university levels who *generally* have doctorate degrees in their fields of expertise with less real world experience. For elementary and secondary school teachers, the college programs offered in teacher education are somewhat similar in nature but vary in structure. Some states require a student to complete a four-year bachelor's degree in their area of expertise first, and then complete a fifth year teacher education certification program. Other states offer a 4-year teacher education Bachelors Degree program combined with a specific area of expertise. There are many other variations of education degree programs; the important point is not so much the variation of the programs, but what is taught and learned about teaching in the program. What is taught and learned in the program directly relates to "student learning" and this is generating the nature of the problem we face.

WHAT TEACHER EDUCATION PROGRAMS TRADITIONALLY FOCUS ON

Aside from all the psychology and behavioral related coursework the programs tend to focus on teacher presentation of material, more often than not, through the traditional methodology of verbal lecture (telling). Education students do study many different teaching methodologies but seem to focus on verbal teaching. In fact, many of the traditional teacher education courses are taught using this method. Again, the programs do teach differing methodologies but actually practice the traditional verbal method of lecture.

Chapter 7: Teacher Education

In contrast, "real world" oriented teachers have been utilizing multi-receptive learning mode teaching for years whereas traditional "liberal arts" teachers too often have not. Many of the "arts" related teachers do not attempt the course pre-preparation and implementation work, incorporating all the receptive learning modes of students, because they lack real world experience of how to apply what they are teaching. This is why so many teachers adopt the textbook method thereby teaching the experience of the author in a verbal format. This is great for "verbal" learning biased students but is disaster for others. Additionally, it becomes habit forming and the teacher builds their whole course around the experience of an author. Traditional teacher education programs promote and rely so strongly on the textbook learning method that they overlook the changing learning needs of the students. That is, the same method will not work for all *environments* including inner city, urban, and rural. In fact, the traditional verbal teaching method is a strong source of the failures, not the answer to the learning problems. Too many of the faculty teaching in the education programs/curriculums are products of the lecture-teach environment and, in essence, are repeatedly teaching what and how they learned. Yes, many will say if was good enough for them, so be it! *Note: It would not be prudent to tell that to the multi-millions of annual dropouts and stay-outs suffering the wrath of traditional "verbal lecture" teaching.*

Ever wonder why the proprietary/private schools are successful? Look at the way they teach math, science, language, etc. Realistically applied, taught utilizing multi-receptive learning modes, by faculty who are experienced in the use of those subjects every day in the real world. And yes, they have similar accreditation as the public schools and colleges. Unfortunately, traditional thinking in some states is quite biased. There are some state education representative's who would prefer to never approve proprietary learning in their state at the "higher degree" level. This perception is why teacher education programs get set on a traditional format and stay there, regardless of need. It appears that technology changes rapidly, including student interest, attention spans, environment, etc., but human nature seems to change little, and in itself, is highly resistant to change. This is the enemy of improvement in teacher education programs and is a major part of the "student learning" problem, not the solution.

WHAT TEACHER EDUCATION PROGRAMS SHOULD FOCUS ON

Simply, teaching teachers how to teach so all students learn! When do teachers know students have learned? Students have learned when:

- They remember it.
- They remember how to do it.
- They do it.
- They repeat it.

Note: the level at which they accomplish these steps will identify their level of learning (example: excellent to poor).

Now again, overall and most important, the teacher's responsibility is "student learning" so they are responsible for *all* their students to:

- Remember it.
- Remember how to do it.
- Do it.
- Repeat it.

So, what should teacher education programs focus on? Initially, teacher education programs must teach prospective teachers how to create and document measurable objectives (what is to be accomplished) for all major topics within a course or topic of study. Subsequent to that, and equally important, how to create and implement multi-receptive learning mode experiences (Hearing, Seeing, Feeling) for those measurable objectives. Multi-receptive learning mode teaching, *for all classes, subjects, and disciplines*, logically increases student learning for *all* students, effecting *all* students to:

- Remember it.
- Remember how to do it.
- Do it.
- Repeat it.

Herein lies the most important operational task of the teacher: to do it! This is what teacher education programs must focus on. Teaching must be based on measurable objectives presented in an *ethical* multi-receptive learning mode format. This should be created and implemented relative to the type and situation of the students, the background and ingenuity of the teacher, the environment, and many other related factors. It is here effective teachers are separated from less effective teachers. Those who can create multi-learning mode experiences accomplishing the four previously noted student outcomes are destined to excel in their profession. Those who cannot could actually deter student learning and inflict perception damage to many. This ability should be decisively improved at the teacher preparation program level.

Textbook note: Most importantly, textbook learning must be reinforced by the teacher's ingenuity to create multivariate learning mode experiences of the textbook author's intentions. *Textbooks are an excellent guide, but the real responsibility for student learning lies with the teacher's interpretation and created learning experiences to accomplish the textbook intentions.*

Interpreting Student Test Results

Tests! To the student, tests means "my grade." To the parents of students it means, "How well they are learning." To the teacher, too often, it means an entry in their grade books and designates who the "good students" are and who the "poor students" are. *In reality, the tests really show the level at which the students learned the material the teacher was teaching, via the method of instruction, and thus is documentation of the teacher's effectiveness.* The teacher must learn from the tests how effective their methods of instruction were and then re-teach, making the necessary instructional improvements to ensure learning.

Think of this: If student test scores are plotted on a graph, grades versus number of students with those grades, the traditionally normal accepted distribution for verbal preach-teaching creates a bell shaped curve. This generally indicates the class has a small number of extreme scores at a high level "A" and a corresponding small number of low scores "F", or so on. The rest cluster in the middle from B's to D's. Therefore, this is, in too many cases, the *accepted* dispersion of grading and even *accepted* to unjustly justify the teacher's proficiency. In too many cases, it is even applied to the overall class test results regardless of overall percentage. What is meant by that? The test may consist of 100 questions and instead of grading based on percentage's (100 percent to 75 percent being acceptable grading, below 75 percent failing) the teachers use the highest number of correct answers in the 100 questions as a starting point instead of 100 percent. Say the students take the test and the best score out of the 100 questions is 60, then that is used as an "A" grade and quite possibly the corresponding "F" might reflect only 30 to 40 right answers out of the 100, dependent on the other scores. Logically that means the real student learning of the 100 questions tested is extremely low, but because of the grading method used, is acceptable and justified. Some cases border on the ridiculous; the best scores are so low the test should never have been given and the student learning of those topics was nil! However, that is/was used and recorded for final grading in the subject, implying satisfactory student learning. The current argument justifying this type of grading process is that the questions are so hard the students are not expected to complete the test so the teacher is finding out the point their students reached in learning the overall material. This is very deceptive! What the teacher really should learn from the grading is the level of learning of the class, thereby documenting his/her teaching effectiveness of the corresponding topic objectives and *what has to be done* to continuously improve learning *for all. If the teacher's responsibility is student learning, then the teacher's responsibility has to be to ensure the learning of those not learning!*

Tests really show how effective the teacher is relative to their student's learning. Yes, many professional teachers will ignore this but if remuneration was dependent upon how much information was received and thus, how well students learned, the professional commitment and teaching methods would likely improve overnight Currently, the overall learning of a class is camouflaged by only publishing individual grades to individual students. The real student learning effectiveness of the teacher is non-transparent and hidden in the class grade book.

The following is an example of a test turned into a learning disaster; This was a college course related to applied mathematics and required the application of trigonometry to solve problems. The teacher would give weekly tests and selected five problems from numerous problems given at the end of each chapter in the course textbook. The teacher gave the weekly test and the five questions were the ones from the text—the students received the results a few days afterward. The result was a "perception of learning" disaster: The whole class received a grade of 100 percent, except for one person who had misplaced a decimal point—one decimal place, on one minor calculation, on one of the five questions. Because of that, and the grading on the curve process, the student "failed" the test and was given an "F" for a weekly grade even though the remainder of his test answers were all 100 percent correct. Think of the perception damage it did to an adult student. Certainly this teacher's perceived job responsibility was to stand in front of the class the student's paid for and sole lecture! In that case he appeared that he could have cared less about who was learning, who was not, and his effect on the adult student's perceptions of the education they were paying for. *This practice should be eliminated from our educational system and the best place to start is in teacher education programs. Focus on student learning with the axiom, "The only failure in the classroom is the teacher."* Eliminate the curve grading process that unjustly justifies the awarding of A's through F's and teach to ensure learning to all in the class. That means teaching to ensure learning that produces a more flat graphical depiction (minimal dispersion) of grades achieved.

Now, in the real world, we cannot expect every student will learn to expectations when we teach to "ensure learning," but logically learning would improve immeasurably over current methodologies and the perception of education would be less threatening, more inviting, and ultimately more effective.

A THOUGHT

Why does the math class failure consistently understand and is able to apply complex odds at the racetrack? Why are computer science failures/dropouts interviewed and employed by major software manufacturers? Why does a science dropout make a major scientific breakthrough? Why are some of our most famous discoveries made by people not related to those specific fields? Why? Because, in the "Real World," necessity has consistently shown that it is the mother of invention. Therefore, teachers, convince students of a realistic necessity to learn that directly and positively interests them and they will ensure their learning, not in spite of you, but because of you!

Improvements: Teacher Education

- ► Learn how to create and document measurable objectives for all major topics within an academic course.
- ► Learn how to test and evaluate student learning (entirely eliminating curve grading) specifically related to course measurable objectives.
- ► Create learning experiences, for all disciplines, ethically utilizing all three modes of learning receptivity that affects the student to: "Remember it, remember how to do it, do it, and repeat it."
- ► Learn how to plan and implement teaching improvement by analyzing the range and dispersion of test grades for individual topic objectives—versus the methods of instruction.
- ► Accept that the most important teaching job responsibility is "student learning."
- ► Display and develop a teaching commitment to the philosophy: "The only failure in the classroom is the teacher."

Chapter 8: Eliminating Gender Bias

Teaching and Gender Bias

Improve teaching and learning for all students by eliminating intentional and unintentional gender bias in schools and colleges.

Unfortunately, "Gender Bias" exists in many forms—in the home, the school, and the workplace. The problem, most importantly in schools, is that the results of gender bias influence the decisions students make in the coursework they take, which in turn influences, and ultimately may limit, their career choices. In reality, this influence is a serious career determining issue and the more we work to eliminate bias the more career opportunities we open to students, regardless of gender.

As to the seeds of gender bias: It appears the shaping of knowledge of one's mind is similar to programming a computer, from birth and on. *"We tend to learn what we live and we live what we learn."* Unfortunately, some positive intentions done as parents, teachers, role models, etc. have unknowing, unrealistic and sometimes negative consequences. This chapter will specifically focus on gender biases from home and in education and their effects.

To begin with, educational investigation indicates there are fewer females in math and science related disciplines specifically because of differences either in: social practices between men and women, the way math and science are taught in elementary and secondary education, traditional advisement in schools, and personal/family obligations. In reality all of these situations appear to contribute to the under-representation of females in science related employment versus their male counterparts.

The social issues begin early in family life with different role expectations between boys and girls. Examples of expectations begin with boys whose expectations are, many times perceived and vocalized by their parents, to grow up to be in more masculine perceived occupations such as builders, tradesmen, engineers, sports players, etc. Whereas girls are many times perceived and vocalized to grow up to be in more "feminine perceived" occupations such as models, nurses, secretaries, elementary school teachers, or less masculine fields. These roles, too many times, are self-fulfilling in that *individuals try to become what is expected of them.*

Unfortunately, what is expected of children is too many times perceived from tradition rather than logical ability. Girls and boys have similar scholastic abilities yet are steered by biases and tradition rather than generated interest. Additional factors relating to the way gender is differentiated are often times related to geographical norms, religious beliefs, family economics, ethnic and racial backgrounds, etc. It appears that all of these factors tend to promote unbalanced career choices resulting in too many students not becoming what they are capable of being, or really interested in being.

Now, going from the home front to school, the gender biases advance and increase seemingly unnoticed but in themselves are a very strong influence in academic course decision making, and thus subsequent career decisions. In education, gender bias tends to begin in the elementary school, continues to the secondary level, and so on. For the most part the coursework developed at these levels is not developed to attract female curiosity. Most lessons presented in the classroom are unknowingly gender biased as historical contributions made by females in science are not emphasized in the curriculum, versus their male counterparts, nor is the course material presented to accommodate the different learning styles of females. The first educational barrier encountered by female students is the challenge of the math and science curriculums. Investigation shows little bias in the early elementary years, but in middle school females begin to show a more negative attitude toward math and science than males.

In reality, females in general have fewer science related experiences than males do. Males have a substantially greater history of working with or fixing something electrical/mechanical than females do. Overall, females are not exposed to toys and activities that ignite their curiosity about science and tend to be less exposed to science in general. This disinterest in science, and resultant math requirements leads females to avoid taking the advanced courses necessary for careers in science. When they graduate from high school, they are not academically equipped or motivated to pursue careers in science or engineering. Therefore, fewer females enroll in science-related programs after they finish high school.

It is logical that to lessen/eliminate gender bias in middle and high school curriculums the teachers need to address the interests and learning styles of females. Additionally, the contributions made by women have to be acknowledged in order to maintain female interest. Herein, as most scientists are male, science traditionally has represented a male point of view. Teaching becomes less gender biased when classroom experimentation focuses more on concerns with social significance and less on specialized mechanical applications. Additionally, solving problems more traditionally female oriented and using less gender biased language allows females to feel less alienated by the process. Examples used in the classroom such as the trajectory of a spacecraft or the mechanical workings of a car are gender biased and few females can relate to the subject matter from prior experience. Because females cannot readily relate to the material, they lose interest and gravitate toward subjects with which they feel more relevance.

Typical advisement in school has its own hidden biases. Studies of junior high school students show too many male and female students are unaware of career options available to them as well as their educational requirements. *Much school advisement and career advisement is predicated on past grades and coursework and this is then used as an inaccurate predictor of future options and success.* Thus, many are counseled into traditional career tracks rather than areas of genuine interest; which would necessitate problem solving with the student on how and what to do to achieve

CHAPTER 8: ELIMINATING GENDER BIAS

career interests and goals. As a former statistics professor once indicated, "National studies conducted to follow students from school to work in order to predict outcomes, based on hundreds of variables, could only reveal with confidence that boys could lift heavier weights than girls." *"Any other variable relationships had minimal significance and were sheer speculation."* Be aware that student advisement based on past performance is time poorly spent. In fact, it is negative because it plants the seed "I can only become something based on what I have already done." This type of thinking has to be abolished in the real world of education and work. Note: people tend to do well what they want to do, and the converse seemingly holds true.

Unfortunately some schools adhered to local and geographical advisement norms such as "boys take shop and girls take home economics." This is a typical example of illogical and gender biased advisement. This practice, occurring in not the too distant past, was practiced by very educated people. Gender bias exists in such simple forms we really do not realize it until we look back and recognize the ignorance of it all. An example: A female student had to get middle-school board approval to take a shop course instead of home economics. The shop course consisted of one semester of mechanical drawing and one semester of hands-on producing what was drawn. It was a personal interest decision that defied local advisement norms and required the permission of the school board and its president. The student was just an average young student who had an interest in mechanical arts instead of home economics. She, after significant persistence, received permission only after getting a male student to agree to take her place in the home economics class. Both students had interests differing from advisement norms. This scenario occurred in a middle school and the female continued through the normal high school curriculum and then went on to college where she received a degree in Mechanical Engineering. Her acceptance of advisement from her college coursework faculty consisted of how to solve the problems related to achieving one's goal, instead of her formal high school adviser's advisement that said: "Your math background is to insufficient in order compete in calculus so try a less demanding career." It is apparent that the middle school "shop course" and her college faculty significantly influenced her career choice and resultant success.

Whether one realizes it or not, most teachers themselves are advising students all the time by their perceived actions, statements, looks, demeanor, biases, etc. Teacher gender in itself is a perceived bias because there are significantly more men teaching in math and science at the college level and females feel in the minority for both support and true "peer" advisement. Classroom climate and a lack of role models all seem to have a negative impact on female science oriented students. At the college level, faculty are often required to conduct research and publish in addition to regular teaching duties, therefore females tend to choose a career in industry because it is more compatible with their family life. That is, companies in the "real world" are more likely to allow women to work part-time. Subsequently, the absence of female faculty for peer support of female science oriented students is a severe detriment to attracting females into science-oriented curriculums. It is a well accepted fact in education that female

CHAPTER 8: ELIMINATING GENDER BIAS

students tend to seek advisement and peer support from female faculty and, because of that relationship, remain in and successfully complete an academic program that they probably would not have, had there been no female support.

As previously described, female students are less likely than men to choose a career in science due to a litany of reasons. Currently females comprise approximately 20 percent of the science and engineering labor force in the U.S. but comprise approximately half the labor force in total. The reasons for this disproportion are certainly diverse but gender bias from home, to and including school, are major factors. So, teachers, just being a teacher has a strong gender impact on the perception of students and carries a professional responsibility to promote knowledge and career opportunities emphasizing gender equality. Again, the only failure to accomplishing this in the classroom can be the teacher.

Note: Chapter 8 Reference: Waldheim, M.L. "Comparison of Female and Male Educators,' Research Proposal Review of Literature—EDD 596, University of Phoenix.

A THOUGHT

Unwitting and common gender bias was demonstrated by an actual phone conversation involving an employee of a parts manufacturing company that was under contract to one of the big three U.S. automakers. The employee called the automaker plant and wanted to discuss an engineering problem they were having with the item they were producing for the plant. The employee transferred by phone tree to the engineering department of the automaker and a *female* voice answered with "Engineering Department, may I help you?" The employee, without hesitation, quickly responded with "I need to talk to an engineer." After a short pause, the *female* voice respectively responded, "I am an engineer." A lengthy pause and an UN-realizing and profound apology.

IMPROVEMENTS: ELIMINATE GENDER BIAS

- ▶ Eliminate language in the classroom that promotes biased perceptions of occupations and successful people by relating to their specific gender.
- ▶ Reduce male gender biased examples used in problem explanations, solutions, and increase female related examples.
- ▶ Increase, earlier in education, career advisement that focuses on UN-biased gender career options and the education requirements to achieve those options.
- ▶ Focus student advisement on what a student wants to do, and how they can do it, rather than what they are limited to because of past performance.
- ▶ Increase female teachers in science and mathematics; serving as both faculty, student mentors, and under-represented role models.
- ▶ Promote female student organizations for traditionally male-dominated curriculums.

Chapter 9: Management of Teachers

The Processes

Improvement in teaching and learning has to be planned, implemented, and then continuously managed by school administration and/or instructional managers in order to be successful.

What is "administration and management?" Well, in practice, someone has to be the leader, the person responsible, or so to speak the manager. In public education, it is called administration. Teachers report to an administrator such as a Department Chair, Department Head, Vice Principle, etc. These positions are generally responsible for the day-to-day management of the faculty. That means being responsible for *faculty/staff hiring and* **evaluation,** *scheduling, meetings, professional development (training), department events, budgeting, etc.*

Evaluation: This is, without a doubt, the most important responsibility of the faculty administrator/supervisor. The evaluation process should document a faculty member's "student learning" effectiveness, and subsequent to that the preparation and implementation of a continuous teaching improvement plan, all relative to the faculty member's reappointment.

A Logical Thought

A continuous faculty evaluation/improvement process, based specifically on the documented level of student learning versus corresponding topic objectives, reveals the effectiveness of a teacher's teaching. The results of this can be analyzed and improvements planned to increase future student learning. *This is generally known as the process of analysis and continuous improvement, though appearing scarce in education, is already well proven in the real world!* Again, the foremost job responsibility of the teacher should be student learning therefore a comprehensive student final examination, or cumulative test grades, should be used to compute a "class grade average" for each course the teacher teaches. This would clearly show the faculty member, administration, and others how well the entire class of students learned the measurable objectives of the course and reveal the effectiveness of the teaching. Again, the documented level of student learning should be the most important criteria in faculty evaluation, along with the faulty member's plan for continuous improvement and their reappointment predicated on the performance of that plan. In agreement, some will say it already is! Conversely, if it really is then all existing faculty would be considered adequately improving and/or excellent—unfortunately the public perception is contrary. How often have you heard or read that a faculty member was released because of poor student learning resulting from poor teaching? Yes, some are released for committing a felony but, for the most part, few faculty members are let go specifically related to *"documented"* poor student learning. That is because *there is not a "somewhat common" system in place to evaluate a faulty member's teaching effectiveness based on their student's learning of topic/course objectives and the teacher's continuous improvement.*

It is public knowledge that our national high school dropout rate is disastrous; the community colleges are filled with students who had poor preparatory learning in high school accompanied by an additional number of prior student "stay-outs" who vowed never to return! However a questionable number of ineffective teachers remain in schools under the premise that acceptable (undocumented) learning takes place. This is an inaccurate premise! It is concerning hearing faculty expound to others they have 20 or so years of experience, implying they are an excellent teacher. In reality, what we realistically have is a teacher with one-year of experience *(not evaluated by how well the students learned the topics he/she was responsible for)* and most often repeated for the next 19 years. This is the nature of the problem and is the breeding ground for an accelerated dropout and stay-out education system. The faculty administrator must be responsible for requiring all faculty to have clearly written measurable course objectives and a comprehensive final examination or cumulative tests to assess student learning of the course objectives. This should be reviewed and approved by the faculty administrator—preferably before the course begins, monitored at specified intervals, and then ultimately utilized to compute the "class grade average," thus documenting the teacher's effectiveness and subsequent methods of instructional improvement.

Final Examinations

It is generally accepted that final examinations should occur at the end of a course of study and the elementary and secondary school systems (responsibility of the state) regularly promote various configurations of that requirement. It is also generally accepted this is not always the case at the post-secondary or college level. Many courses of study at the college level forgo a final examination, growing numbers to the extent that one regional accreditation commission now requires a "culminating experience" at the end of each course. Herein lies the problem: In order to document the effectiveness of the teaching we have to determine the level of learning of the students. A most logical and ethical way is to have a comprehensive examination at the end of each course which is based on the measurable objectives of the course. How can a teacher improve if they do not know what they have accomplished, and/or how effective they are? In short, it should be required of all public learning institutions that comprehensive final examinations or cumulative interval tests (based on *all* course measureable objectives) occur for *all* students enrolled in a course. No student exceptions, no exemptions, etc.

The implementation of this process must be the responsibility of the faculty administrator. It is the very foundation of continuous improvement, both for the teacher and the students. Be aware that improvement in education, or any organization, does not just happen. It is developed through a process of analysis and continuous improvement until the organization reaches the point its performance is publicly recognized to be better than anyone else and it becomes the leader by recognition. Without continuous improvement the contrary tends to occur!

CURRENT FACULTY EVALUATION

Unfortunately, the most common faculty evaluation process tends to *minimally* review the student grade picture derived from final examinations or other cumulative student testing. Why? Many courses do not have clearly written and measurable topic objectives. Those courses taught from a textbook can utilize the text chapter objectives, but a course final examination or cumulative tests should be developed to comprehensively measure the student achievement of those objectives, and to determine the effectiveness of the teaching. Where there are few written and measurable objectives it is next to impossible to clearly analyze student learning, and the level of learning of those objectives. Therefore, what might be reviewed are the final course grades from the final course grade sheets submitted by the teacher. This hardly indicates the level of student learning of specific course objectives unless the teacher has the evaluation instruments (the tests) tied to each course objective. There are instances where teachers might practice this process but, for the most part, the final grades reflect accumulated quizzes, documents, rewards, and the results of a generalized final test, if it is given at all.

The major problem is that teachers are not evaluated critically on the learning level of their students because, in too many cases, there are no measurable objectives tied to evaluative tests for the topics the teacher is teaching. *This situation appears to be more prevalent at the college level.* Even if there were credible tests for the subjects the teacher is teaching, the reappointment of the teacher by administration would and could not be determined on that data. Why? Because faculty evaluation is generally so skewed by other evaluative factors that student learning, if documented at all, would only be a small fractional part of the overall review. Again, where or when have you heard of a faculty member being required to improve, or released, because of poor student learning? Unfortunately, the system is ingrained in a teacher evaluation process that *unwittingly* protects poor faculty performance and thus resists improvement attempts by administrators and/or instructional managers. Had faculty been contractually responsible for student learning and the standardized test or other test results tied to measurable objectives revealed student learning was at an unacceptable level, the administration would at least have documentation to support necessary improvement. In many cases a faculty member has continuing reappointment because of tenure status, *is not contractually responsible for documenting student learning and/or improvement,* and the school system (given the legal roadblocks) would not even attempt requiring improvement. Therefore, poor teaching continues, students drop out, and the public wonders why our schools have the problems that they have. So, the government legislates more money into the system (programs, initiatives, etc.) and winds up with the same result. That is why legislating more money into an operationally deficient system will not work. The current public educational system needs change and improvement to function *for* the real world. It is apparent that operationally our current public educational *system* unintentionally and illogically protects poor teaching that results in poor student learning. This is just the opposite of what reasonable parents, taxpayers, educational leaders, or interested people want. *To have accountability in the teaching system teachers must be accountable for their job responsibility, specifically "student learning." Then, measure their effectiveness by documenting and analyzing the student learning that took place. Based on that analysis, make changes to improve future student learning (improving the methods of instruction) and continue the process as the major part of a faculty member's annual evaluation.* This, initially, might be a resisted practice because it is intimidating the status-quo. Fortunately there are teachers who would welcome it, do not see it as intimidation, because their teaching goal is "student learning." If their students were not learning, the way they wanted them to, they would make immediate improvements in order to have their students learn. Anything less would be an insult to their ability—*they are the few and the proud!* It is public knowledge that many parents, students, educators, lawmakers and other critics of education do not support the teaching and resultant learning practices in the current system. They see the resultant deficiencies but are restricted by rules and negotiated contractual terms appearing too demonstrable to change.

Important Concepts

Begin with accepting the concept the most important person in the classroom is the student—what they learn, and at what level they learn. Most will acknowledge the student is the most important person, but the real issue will be "at what level they learn." This will be resisted with the perpetual argument: "teachers have no control over the student's level of learning," "Teachers teach and it is up to the students as individuals to learn." This argument leads to teacher complacency, apathy, and is the major problem we face, not the solution. The good teachers have the common goal of student learning as their main purpose in the classroom. Not because someone told them to, but because they believe it is their professional responsibility as a teacher. This seems to be the common value of those teachers who receive awards for excellent teaching. So then, what and at what level the students learn should be the primary concern of everyone. That primary concern must be the primary responsibility of the employed teacher. Being the primary responsibility, the teacher should be evaluated on their student's documented level of learning. To do this, many current accepted practices will have to improve. Documented measurable topic objectives in all courses, comprehensive testing of the objectives to document student learning, and teacher evaluation based on the level of student learning that took place and a process of continuous improvement.

Contrary to the advocates of the current system, there are no measurable topic objectives in all courses, we do not have comprehensive testing of objectives (some yes but far from all), and certainly teacher evaluation *is not* based on a documented level of student learning and continuous improvement. This concept of documenting student learning does not take away the freedom of the curriculum designers or specialty offerings of differing schools, it only holds the teachers, administration, and schools accountable for their responsibility of student learning.

Because the public is ultimately paying the teacher's salaries, and students make the effort to go to school, students and the public want to be confident they are going to learn! In the "real world," this is more than reasonable and just makes sense. Everything contrary to this is just verbiage and has put the burden of the production of the product on the consumer, the student, instead of the product producer, the school and teacher. It is difficult to believe and/or justify why common sense logic in education evolved years ago from *"pay for what you receive"* to now *"pay in spite of what you receive"* and deftly persists in our business oriented society. This **perception** has to reverse itself in order for the United States to become a real world leader in education. *The public has to be convinced and satisfied that it is getting value for their money. The operational process of analysis and continuous improvement is proven world-wide to accomplish just that.*

A THOUGHT

A most important question schools should answer about student learning is: What is the *minimum acceptable* level of student learning as determined by a comprehensive final examination or cumulative testing "class grade average" for classes taught at the institution? How is it determined, documented, made public, and then analyzed in the faculty reappointment process.

Now, how often or when has the public ever seen the total spread of final examination grades for an entire class? Forget about student names, just the final examination grades or cumulative test grades for all students in the class and, collectively, how that depicts the overall level of learning taking place in the class? Never published, never talked about, never, whatever! It is apparent that the time is arriving where public leaders will request/demand schools to publish their teacher's effectiveness for individual classes so the taxpayers and potential students see what they will be getting for their money. Yes, the taxpayers and students are actually paying the salaries of the public school's faculty, staff, and administrators even though the dollars go through a convoluted evolution of fiscal dispersal. What difference would it make to hand the actual remuneration money to the faculty, staff, and administrators (all in person) after the course was completed? The institutions would certainly respond more positively to personal financial confrontation and become less defensive and more "amenably motivated." Because this will probably not occur in our complex system, we must have a built in mandate of "continuous improvement" (as previously described) to counter complacency and its various viruses, enabling education to function in the real world where strong performance and value predicts success.

Improvements: Management of Teachers

- Document and make publicly available all faculty class grade averages and resultant levels of teaching effectiveness (derived by final examinations or cumulative tests) for the most recent classes taught.

- Determine the learning institution's minimally acceptable "class grade average" for student learning and teaching effectiveness.

- Ensure all faculty have clearly written measureable objectives for all major course topics and comprehensive final examinations or cumulative tests to assess student learning of those objectives.

- Ensure comprehensive final examinations or cumulative tests take place for all classes and a subsequent "class grade average" is documented, to grade the level of student learning and resultant teaching effectiveness.

- Ensure all faculty, for every contract period (*at least annually*) prepare an acceptable continuous teaching improvement plan by analyzing the range and dispersion of test grades for individual topic objectives—versus the methods of instruction .

- Ensure that all faculty re-appointment contracts are subject to attaining an acceptable level of teaching effectiveness (class grade average) and a continuous improvement teaching plan.

Chapter 10: Ethics and Teaching

Responsibilities

Improve teaching and learning in schools and colleges by practicing and being an ethically responsible professional.

In the real world "ethics" are perceived as practicing good conduct and having moral principles or values. More accurately the dictionary defines it as the *"rules or standards governing the conduct of members of a profession."* This definitely relates to the teaching profession and thus directly affects student learning. The effect that a teacher's ethics has on the perceptions learned by students is prolific. One only has to read and study the written student evaluations of faculty to realize the profound affect the values of the teacher has on the perception of the students. It is generally discussed by students that there are few classes taken where the teacher's political views and other personal values have not been forthcoming. Some to the outright extent that it could clearly affect one's relationship with the teacher and subsequently one's perception of the grade received. Faculty projection of personal/political/religious views is a breeding ground for deceptive learning and must be eliminated from the learning environment.

It is well accepted in the education profession that the teacher is the leader in the classroom and must conduct themselves at the highest level of perceived values. Remember students are learning from the teacher's perceived actions as well as their words. Personal views and actions relating to religion, politics, morality, and other controversially potential subjects should be avoided unless they are an integral part of the course being taught. **Where controversial subjects are a required part of the course, and discussed, it is the teacher's responsibility to present both sides of the issue with the intent of providing enough non-biased information so students can make their own judgments and decisions in a non-biased atmosphere.**

In practice it appears that "ethics" seems to be a subject in teaching practice and evaluation that is generally avoided until a problem occurs and then pundits refer to the obvious "ethical professional responsibility" of the person or whatever in question; after the fact. Relative to this there was strong discussion within at least one regional accreditation commission that "ethics" should be a required course in all college professional programs but that gained little support because it would require lengthening the program of study which is not a popular topic. The substitute to an actual new course was the accepted notion that "ethics" is a subject already "embedded" in the curriculum. This meant that teachers discuss ethics as the need arises within the various courses of the curriculum. However experience indicates that this does not appear to be effective, in light of the published number of professional teacher violations relating to unethical conduct. One only has to read the continual media reports of public teachers being involved in conduct contrary to their professional responsibilities. This type of non-ethical behavior has no place in education because it is the teacher's professional responsibility to *always* set a positive example of character and values.

The following description just about sums up "ethics" in education. A teacher must be both a manager and a leader. The manager of the classroom environment and the leader of the subject/group being taught. The ethical responsibilities of both positions are well defined by the paraphrase: "Managers must do things right—Leaders must do the right things."

IMPROVEMENTS: ETHICS AND TEACHING

- Ensure that faculty are aware they have a professional responsibility and are accountable to conduct themselves at the highest level of perceived values.

Chapter 11: Improving Schools and Colleges

To: Parents, Students, Educators, Lawmakers, and the General Public:

Question: *What type of school would you choose? One that tells you what you are going to learn and the effectiveness of the teaching—all before you pay? Or, the current contrary!* **Choice can be a reality when schools adopt and implement the following improvements:**

Current Teaching and Learning (Chapter 1)

- Teachers and administrators accept responsibility and accountability for analyzing student learning for improvement of instruction.
- Limit selective teaching by "verbal lecture" (expounding, urging, telling).
- Teach by ethically utilizing all three modes of learning receptivity for all course objectives.

- Develop student interest in all the subjects taught in the classroom.
- Promote student accomplishment for all students in the classroom.
- Measure, grade, and analyze student learning thus documenting teacher effectiveness.

Teacher Responsibility and Accountability
(Chapter 2)

- Accept personal and professional responsibility for student learning.
- Inspire student motivation and generate a cause to learn for all course topics.
- Create measureable objectives for all major course topics.
- Teach by ethically utilizing all three modes of learning receptivity for all course objectives.
- Document a "class grade average," grading the level of learning of all course measureable objectives and resultant teaching effectiveness, for each assigned course.
- Compute the "class grade average," using comprehensive final examination grades or cumulative test grades; all enrolled students—no exemptions.
- Prepare a continuous teaching improvement plan by analyzing the range and dispersion of class test grades for individual topic objectives—versus the methods of instruction.

CHAPTER 11: IMPROVING SCHOOLS AND COLLEGES

Teaching Methodologies (Chapter 3)

- Ethically incorporate all three receptive learning modes for teaching all course measurable objectives.

- Create genuine student interest in all course objectives and abolish threats of failure or threats of any kind.

- Create intermittent course tests to measure student learning and evaluate teaching effectiveness of all major course objectives. Utilize the results for the improvement of instruction, such as re-teaching, versus student grading.

- Display a recognizable classroom attitude and demeanor that the teacher's primary priority is "student learning."

Teacher Preparation (Chapter 4)

- Divide all major course information into measureable Topic Objectives.

- Determine multi-mode Methods of Instruction for each Topic Objective.

- Analyze learning (the dispersion of test grades) of all Topic Objectives.

- Improve the Methods of Instruction based on the Analysis of Learning.

- Create a one page Learning Plan for each Topic Objective stating: the Topic Objective, Methods of Instruction, Analysis of Learning, and Improvements.

- Amend the Learning Plan sections; "Analysis of Learning" and "Improvements" on a continual basis—each time the Topic Objective is taught.

Teacher Evaluation (Chapter 5)

- Document measurable course objectives for all major course topics taught.
- Document comprehensive final examinations and/or cumulative tests that include all major course measurable objectives, for all courses taught.
- Document a "class grade average for each assigned course, grading the class level of learning and resultant teaching effectiveness.
- Compute the "class grade average" using the comprehensive final examination grades or cumulative test grades: all enrolled students, no exemptions.
- Prepare a continuous teaching improvement plan by analyzing the range and dispersion of test grades for individual topic objectives—versus the methods of instruction.
- Demonstrate re-appointment based on acceptable class grade averages in the most recent classes, and an acceptable continuous teaching improvement plan.

Teacher Contracts (Chapter 6)

- Identify all courses the teacher is assigned to teach.
- Require preparation of measurable objectives for all major topics in each course assigned.
- Require comprehensive final course examinations that include all major course measurable objectives, for all students enrolled in all courses assigned, no exemptions.
- Document a "class grade average," grading the level of

learning of all course measureable objectives and resultant teaching effectiveness, for each assigned course.

▶ Compute the "class grade average," using comprehensive final examination grades or cumulative test grades; all enrolled students, no exemptions.

▶ Demonstrate an acceptable level of teaching effectiveness based on the most recent "class grade averages."

▶ Prepare a continuous improvement teaching plan by analyzing the range and dispersion of test grades for individual topic objectives—versus the methods of instruction.

▶ Receive, for contract reappointment, approval of all aforementioned requirements.

Teacher Education (Chapter 7)

▶ Learn how to create and document measurable objectives for all major topics within an academic course.

▶ Learn how to test and evaluate student learning (entirely eliminating curve grading) specifically related to course measurable objectives.

▶ Create learning experiences, ethically utilizing all three modes of learning receptivity for all disciplines, that affects the student to: "Remember it, remember how to do it, do it, and repeat it."

▶ Learn how to generate continuous teaching improvement by analyzing the range and dispersion of test grades for individual topic objectives—versus the methods of instruction.

▶ Accept that the most important teaching job responsibility is "student learning."

- Display and develop a teaching commitment to the philosophy: "The only failure in the classroom is the teacher."

Eliminating Gender Bias (Chapter 8)

- Eliminate language in the classroom that promotes biased perceptions of occupations and successful people by relating to their specific gender.
- Reduce male gender biased examples used in problem explanation and solutions, and increase female related examples.
- Increase, earlier in education, career advisement that focuses on UN-biased gender career options and education requirements to achieve those options.
- Focus student advisement on what a student wants to do, and how they can do it, rather than what they are limited to because of past performance.
- Increase female teachers in science and mathematics, serving as faculty, student mentors, and under-represented role models.
- Promote female student organizations for traditionally male-dominated curriculums.

Management of Teachers (Chapter 9)

- Document and make publicly available all faculty member's class grade averages and resultant levels of teaching effectiveness (derived by final examinations or cumulative tests) for the most recent classes taught.
- Determine the learning institution's minimally

acceptable "class grade average" for student learning and teaching effectiveness.

▶ Ensure all faculty, for all courses, have clearly written measureable objectives for all major course topics and comprehensive final examinations or cumulative tests assessing student learning of those objectives.

▶ Ensure comprehensive final examinations or cumulative tests take place for all classes and a subsequent "class grade average" is documented, to grade the level of student learning and resultant teaching effectiveness.

▶ Ensure all faculty, for every contract period, *at least annually,* prepare an acceptable continuous teaching improvement plan by analyzing the range and dispersion of test grades for individual topic objectives—versus the methods of instruction.

▶ Ensure that all faculty re-appointment contracts are subject to attaining an acceptable level of teaching effectiveness (class grade average) and a continuous improvement teaching plan.

Ethics and Teaching (Chapter 10)

▶ Ensure that faculty are aware they have a professional responsibility and are accountable to conduct themselves at the highest level of perceived values.

A Final Thought

The Beginning of this Story started in the "Real World" because, in the real world, experience has demonstrated that holding the creator/producer of a product accountable for the performance of the product—ensures its performance.

Imagine an auto producer who did not have to be accountable for the cars they produce. The public would probably be driving lower quality, high emissions vehicles that are more dangerous compared to the current vehicles; the responsibility for which is held accountable by purchasers, consumer groups, numerous related agencies, and courts of law. What is probably just as notorious as a non-accountable product producer is a publicly funded education system that is not specifically accountable for the most important product it produces—"student learning." In the "real world" analysis and continuous improvement are most logically derived from and applied to the product produced. In education *analysis* and *continuous improvement* are inconsequential because they are not derived from and applied to "student learning." It is conceivable that if education has survived this long without documenting and analyzing student learning, *specifically for the sake of continuous improvement,* think of what we would be able to accomplish with an educational system committed to the aforementioned practices.

In any established organization, a change, or more particularly an improvement process, is "a hard pill to swallow." "It has been done this way for years and it has worked out O.K.—why change now?" So look around! Is what you see the same as in previous years? In current times concepts, products, media, and the *human response to change* evolves so fast it is hard to keep abreast of even the language that accompanies the change. The reality is if the world of education does not move with it, those in the business of public education will be, *and are*, in the business of losing business. The invitation to, and the attractiveness of, proprietary/independent learning in our country, in just the last few years, has been phenomenal. It is too easy to feel job-protected when you are employed by a characteristically "slow to respond" protective giant institution like a city, county, or state. But, *when the public* seriously begins to question the producers of the educational product, because there are obvious problems with the product (mediocre ranking, excessive drop-outs, expressive stay-outs, low SAT scores etc.), **the public will look for, and purchase, a different product elsewhere.**

Therefore, leaders who commit to "Improving Teaching and Learning in Schools and Colleges" will ultimately be those who specifically want the best education we can provide for *"all"* of our students. Unfortunately, promoting new programs, initiatives, and incentives in our system is an annual never-ending debate of proposed solutions to our education problems. *Yet in spite of these genuinely motivated endeavors* **significant improvement is not forthcoming!** For the United States to be a world leader in education, educators must take the reformation lead in being accountable for their major job responsibility—student learning. *This means documenting the level of student learning and practicing a subsequent process of analysis and continuous improvement.* This is the most important step in "Improving Teaching and Learning in Schools and Colleges." Everything after that, improvements acknowledged herein, are merely *"academic."*

That's the End of the Story

www.ingramcontent.com/pod-product-compliance
Lightning Source LLC
Chambersburg PA
CBHW021954090426
42811CB00001B/26